MONEY HOAX

CHERYL BYFIELD

ACKNOWLEDGEMENTS

My first expression of gratitude is to God, Creator of all worlds, who gives wisdom, knowledge and understanding to all who ask.

My heartfelt appreciation goes to my daughter Otsanya ("OT"), my supporters, cheerleaders and others who made it possible for me to research, write and share this publication.

Although blind and partially deaf, "OT", you are my biggest source of inspiration. You taught me never to give up on any dream. You showed me what determination to survive means, taught me to be strong and be patient. You possess such strong will! You captivated me with your thoughts expressed in music on the keyboard, especially those moments when you would play repetitively to get it right. Your countless pats on my back, your kind, calm, gentle spirit, love, and patience motivated and kept me going.

Thanks to those supporters who wrestled with me in conversations on the topics of money and economics. Your perspectives on the potential of money to make or break the family unit, to build or tear down relationships and its negative bearing on sex, religion, friendships, and work ethics, helped to unravel and shape my presentation.

Thanks to my key supporter Gregory, whose reasonings were grounded in truth, and who sensed that urgent need to continue building awareness for change. Your reasonings provided solid encouragement.

Thanks to my cheerleaders. You know who you are. I will always cherish your knowledge and wit.

THOUGHTS & PHILOSOPHY

The individual is the collective,
balance the individual and balance the collective.
Engage the mind of the individual and engage the collective minds.
Bring harmony to the individual and harmonize the collective minds.
A compassionate individual first, then a compassionate collective.
Love from the individual will give love to the collective.
"Do unto others as you would have them do unto you." When the
individual practices critical thinking,
the collective demonstrates sensitivity.
When the individual wishes good for oneself, the collective has no
choice but to do likewise.
The individual makes the collective.

"Until we transition from a monetary based economic system to a
collaborative work based economic system, I too like all others, continue the struggle to earn money; hopefully
enough to adequately acquire water, food, shelter, and clothing.

Be transformed as you read!

CONTENTS

PART 1: THE JOURNEY...1

PART 2: ECONOMIC SYSTEMS AND THEIR IMPACTS ON OUR LIVES ... 10

PART 3: COMPETITION THE HUGE EVIL 36

PART 4: SCARCITY AND ELIMINATING IT 49

PART 5: DOES GOD LOVE YOU? 69

PART 6: THE HE DOMINANCE.............................83

PART 7: WHAT IS GOOD? 132

ADDENDUM 178

PART 1: THE JOURNEY

Life is a journey. It is filled with challenges, excitement, and surprises, and becomes rather colorful quite frequently. One looks at the birth of an idea, any idea, or a dream. It will undergo outside scrutiny and criticisms, then gradually assume new status.

One looks at the sunset and wonders whether the dream disappears below the setting sun. It is not lost. It is about to experience change of place for another light. It sets, it rests, and it reappears to brighten a new day. Some may say it regenerates and rejuvenates.

The idea, which is supposed to be a solution to a problem, assumes a new status. Suddenly it becomes motivated, it is bright and attractive as it illuminates and surges upward like a tree in rapid growth. Having established a foundation, it is now full speed ahead to beyond the sunset. Such speed takes on new challenges. However, in solving one problem, others originate. The appearance of a color wheel bears some similarity as the mixing of one color with other results in other colors.

One cannot take them all on. There must be separations as some things need to be left behind for success to be a reality. However, what is left behind oftentimes receives new energy, and is nurtured taking on new dimensions. It is like the magnificent view of the sun setting on the shores of the sea, traveling beyond and yet sending those radiant reflections on the ocean providing a path that connects.

Like the processes involved in idea generation, selection and implementation, my life's journey has been a mix of experiences ranging from the humble lifestyle that I enjoyed while growing up in the district of Bottom Ivy in St. Catherine, Jamaica, the challenges of caring for a daughter with special needs, to financial problems exacerbated by a desire for academic excellence and achievement of my professional goal to become an architect.

MY LIFE IN BOTTOM IVY

I am a Jamaican citizen by birth. I was born at the Linstead Hospital in St. Catherine on May 10, 1965; the second of two girls for my mother who was a single parent. We lived in a district called Bottom Ivy, located approximately four miles outside the town of Ewarton in the parish of St. Catherine. Mom was a dressmaker. She used her dressmaking skills to provide financial support for my sister and I right up to our high school years. She was also a Seventh Day Adventist; hence, we grew up on the values and principles of the Seventh Day Adventist denomination.

At our home in Bottom Ivy, we lived simple but intense lives, despite not having the most abundant, and widely used, life-sustaining substance on Earth piped to our home. Water is indeed life, and without easy access to the clean, fresh liquid over extended periods, we suffered many inconveniences. However, the rain and three springs located near to our home, served as a source of water for many years.

The carrying of water on my head was most necessary for our survival especially during some periods of low rainfall. I fetched water early mornings and in the evenings after school. Many times, I increased the volume by carrying other containers, one in each hand, which created a nice balance. No doubt, this caused me added stress and contributed to the frequent bouts of migraine I endured for many years. We fetched water for drinking from a ground spring called Whalley Spring at a neighbor's property approximately a mile away. Frogs enjoyed the spring water just as much as we did. They were a permanent fixture and had no problem sharing the water. Whalley Spring still serves as a reliable water source today. From time to time, we would also utilize two other flowing springs further away, but primarily for doing our laundry. The flow was heavy and there were tiki tiki fish at some points that made those wash days exciting. Sometimes we carried drinking water in smaller bottles when we traveled to the town of Ewarton.

Electricity was not available in our district; hence we utilized lamps, candles, and flashlights at night. We were very keen on replenishing our supply of Berec batteries to power up our radio. Many thanks to the inventors of radios with batteries, because listening to West Indies Cricket and many other radio programs was simply spectacular for me.

I enjoyed star gazing and was a lover of the moon especially when it was it was a full moon, illuminating the night sky. The twinkling stars always held me spellbound. I would often try to count as many as I could. I could not help but thank and worship the awesome God, Creator of the awesome heaven and Earth.

At Bottom Ivy, there was an abundant supply of ground provisions at home and on other distant family-owned properties, which we subsisted on. We raised common fowls for meat consumed mostly on Sundays and Mondays. Cow's milk was also a popular Sunday morning treat. Cornmeal porridge and turn cornmeal were weekday favorites, so was bush tea. We used mint, spirit weed, soursop leaves and cerasee for tea quite frequently. We also had various fruit trees to subsist on and we regularly shared different food items and fruits with our neighbors. We had excellent neighbors in the community.

Our outdoor kitchen, which was located approximately fifteen feet from the house, was used mostly during daytime. Food and vegetables that required refrigeration would be stored on an outdoor table in the cool of the night. At the dawn of day, the overnight dew would manifest in fresh droplets of water on the leafy vegetables, the carrots, sweet peppers, and other food items.

We had a reasonably well-maintained pit latrine for sanitary conveniences, which stood approximately 30 feet away from our wattle and daub house. However, we had an enemy in the very tiny, red "pity mi likkle" ants, which frequently presented on the red polished wooden toilet seat and spared no pity in their bites.

I received primary education at Ewarton Primary School and secondary education at Charlemount High School, where I have fond memories in music and even sports. I was a long-distance runner, running all the distances and always having to settle for second place.

Over the years, our entire living, and outdoor quarters, except the pit latrine, deteriorated under hard times and eventually disintegrated. Unfortunately, water is still not piped to the property. Rainwater is therefore collected, stored in drums, and used mostly for cooking, washing, and drinking to a lesser extent. The land remains productive, and a caretaker maintains the property.

The lack of piped water in Bottom Ivy is not unique. Many communities today, too numerous to count are still suffering the inconveniences of not having easy access to water. Sadly, very little improvements have occurred to provide the ever-increasing population with the liquid, and it appears there will be no change for generations to come. What was lacking then, to give citizens constant access to water, is still lacking today, and will be lacking tomorrow.

LIFE IN KINGSTON, JAMAICA

I relocated to Kingston after graduating from high school in the eighties and life has been very different from living in Bottom Ivy. I cannot even recall a hot night back then when I think of how hot it has progressively become since I relocated to Kingston. I do not recall ever going to bed hungry, as I have had to endure, several times during my years in Kingston city.

In 2003, I commenced further studies at the Caribbean School of Architecture, University of Technology, Jamaica (UTECH). I graduated in 2007 earning my Bachelor of Arts degree with Honors in Architectural Studies.

Meeting my financial needs was challenging. Over a three-year period, I sold all the furniture I owned to help with my college financing. I also moved out of my home and rented same to obtain an income.

My final year at the Caribbean School of Architecture (2006-2007) was the toughest of the four years. I remembered balancing classes with frequent visits to the University Hospital of the West Indies, to assist with the post- operative care for my daughter, Otsanya ("OT") who was born in 1993 and has special needs.

I moved into a rented one-bedroom flat in August Town at the beginning of my final year at UTECH. It was close enough to the University and the rent was affordable considering the little I had. It meant very little traveling and I could save on petrol. Food was however a scarce commodity, just as money was scarce in our hands. If gunshots were edible, I might not have experienced hunger. It was readily accessible based on the frequent firepower that would occur in the area where I resided.

People thought that I was crazy to live at the bottom of Gold Smith Villa, which was near the base of the feared Jungle 12 gang in August Town, but that was the best I could have done under the circumstances. I knew very well that the good and the bad were everywhere. However, I was convinced that the worst does not necessarily reside in the ghetto. I survived cross firing of gunshots just a little over a year after moving to Gold Smith Villa. On occasion, shots were discharged in very close proximity. There were quiet times too. I would try to get home before 8:30 p.m. each night as I was advised to do. There were a few nights when 10:00 p.m. and in one instance 11:00 p.m. caught me on campus. I drove home repeating softly, quietly, "Lord I did not do this on purpose, so will you take me home safely."

I remembered being awakened one night by the sound of very heavy breathing inside my bedroom. I jumped up and said madly, "Get out of here you are already dead." The following morning, I asked a neighbor if anyone was killed inside the yard. I did not get an answer.

When Hurricane Dean blew in late 2008, I never thought my daughter and I would have made it unscathed as the wind and rain pounded the roof. Fortunately, the whole roof stayed on. Just at the point when there appeared a leak from the roof onto my study desk it was all over. A few days after the hurricane, I moved back to occupy two rooms that became vacant at my home. Nevertheless, sometimes I really do miss living in August Town. The flat I rented was close to a steep hill and walking up the hill with my daughter was very good exercise for both of us. I was not deterred by the history of gunfight and death. People died everywhere. Every morning, the dew outside my flat was simply awesome, and I was reminded of the early morning dew at my childhood home. I used the dew to wash my car several mornings. Yes, it was that much; fresh, clean, and awesome.

After completing UTECH, I returned to my old job which I had left to pursue further studies. Although I was doing very well bringing in business for the company, breaking sales records and rewriting new records which the business owner thought was fantastic, they decided to resort to a rather strange way of compensating salespersons by introducing a new remuneration package. This would literally ensure that some earnings would be returned to the company over time, and one could end up owing the employer.

It reminded me of the strange and ridiculous new law that Daniel in the Bible was exposed to during the era of the Babylonians. For thirty days, anyone who worshipped any other god or man other than the king would be thrown into the lion's den. Imagine throwing another human to be eaten by lions simply for doing good, serving God, and having a difference of opinion. That was the trigger, which led me to pursue higher education at the University of Technology.

I started working at age 18 years, months after I graduated from Charlemount High School and except on Saturdays, I have never stopped working. By the standards of some, life has passed me by times over especially with having to take care of my special need's child. However, I have tried to remain steadfast, trusting God for guidance, care, and protection especially over my daughter. I knew something was totally wrong about continuously working for money which was never available in the amounts necessary to attend to the most basic recurring need for food, water, and shelter. I also knew there must be a better way. I was determined to find it as my financial situation continued to spiral downwards with challenges in repaying students' loan and in meeting my mortgage commitments.

Before attending UTECH, I had very good credit ratings. I was also heavily taxed. In fact, in 2003 my tax payment exceeded J$430,000. In 2002 it exceeded J$300,000 and was also high in other years. Consider if I had a tax rebate of say J$500,000 and not students' fake loan, I would have been spared the overwhelmingly burdensome fake debt to repay. (See the meaning of fake loan in the addendum.) The wise man Solomon said, "A false balance is abomination to the Lord, but a just weight is his delight" (Proverbs 11:1). The Students' Loan Bureau claimed they loaned me a little over J$400,000 fake money and with interest which is money that is non- existent, my total repayment when completed was more than J$1,100,000. I made a huge mistake and invested J$200,000 actual currency in the failed Cash Plus scheme to assist with the servicing of the Students' Loan Bureau's fake loan. That cash died but is not resting in peace. How stupid can one get due to lack of knowledge?

Getting my mortgage payment back in line with the Victoria Mutual Building Society (VMBS) was a huge challenge, having fallen in arrears more than J$150,000. By June 2007, they had no interest in the fact that I successfully completed University and had a job and a job letter as proof of income, to negotiate for refinancing and debt consolidation. My total indebtedness to the society was a little over J$3.5 million and the value of my house at the time was J$7 million dollars. I also had a loan and a credit card with a limit of J$230,000 from the Bank of Nova Scotia (BNS). I owed BNS approximately J$243,000 on the credit card. My overall liability at both VMBS and BNS was J$4.6 million.

At VMBS, I cried in the mortgage manager's office when she told me that there was absolutely nothing, they could do to grant me refinancing. They told me that they were answerable to the Bank of Jamaica whose auditors would certainly not be pleased with refinancing such delinquency. Such was the explanation given. They would never let you know that loan defaults and bankruptcies are in fact built into the evil monetary systems of mortgages and loans, and are unavoidable, hence discretion could easily apply. I had previously written unanswered letters to the society about my upcoming financial difficulties and asked whether they could consider giving me a moratorium. Follow-up visits and telephone calls in search of a reply got me answers such as my situation did not warrant such considerations. I was told to sell the house and pay up. Imagine I was to sell the house, become homeless and VMBS, a financial entity, was to be given the proceeds of the sale. Do you think that banks or building societies use money to control lives?

I set out in search of refinancing assistance. I first went to CIBC First Caribbean International Bank in New Kingston, and I was referred to their building society department, where another lady scolded me for taking such a daring risk to attend college full time. I was told that I was irresponsible, and the building society could not risk their money with someone like me. I was very intimidated to approach the Bank of Nova Scotia because my credit card, another fake indebtedness was with them. Money can indeed drive fear causing one to feel helpless and hopeless. Nonetheless, I made an appointment. I was told my indebtedness to BNS would not allow them to offer me any additional assistance and therefore I should settle my outstanding debt with the bank as soon as possible. Jamaica National Building Society needed over J$200,000 actual cash up front in closing costs etc. If I had that cash, I would not have needed them and possibly could have brought my payments up to date with VMBS.

I concluded that taking risks and making sacrifices for higher education was really a bad decision on my part. My situation was made worse since I had a child who was challenged mentally, visually and in need of ear surgery. For me it was all about taking care of her, providing her with a home and being able to take care of her medical expenses. I questioned, "How do I survive this?"

My next and final stop was with Churches Co-operative Credit Union now First Heritage Co-operative Credit Union on Eureka Road. My interaction on this occasion was with a man who appeared less robotic than the women at all the other places combined. I concluded several years later that these women all interacted like robots. Although perhaps well intentioned, their freewill and creativity were under permanent hypnosis. The policies they were guided by had fulfilled its design to manipulate and control minds to defend money over human. They have multiplied tremendously since 2008. Men have no fear in breaking and manipulating their own policies, systems, and oppressive laws. However, they can depend on women to be robots. Women wanted to appear tough. Today they are.

The man at the credit union gave me some hope albeit temporary. He assured me that the credit union would help, which they did. However, the calculations for my mortgage payments, property insurance and students' loan exceeded J$100,000 per month. With food, utilities, car maintenance and other expenses not included, I swear I was going to develop cancer. You had better believe that financial stress is the gateway to many, many illnesses.

The first pay package from my job qualified me for the loan. However, that changed as the owners revised the figures saying the first offer was an error. I had to work with it, and I kept doing my usual repetitive work making sure that before 3:30 p.m. I collected my daughter from the School of Hope, taking her back to the office with me. However, the income was never enough and has never been enough, not for me not for anyone.

So, the days of mortgage arrears returned, and the letters of demand started coming once more. Guess who became the fire under my tail? It was another tough robot.

I registered a business, AC&S Architects, and did much to attract clients. I ventured into furniture designs and met with some success. I had an excellent carpenter; however, work ethics was missing, and I again lacked the cash for investment in the business. I worked at getting construction projects and thought that getting started with government contracts would be a great option. I applied for and received my Tax Compliance Certificate (TCC). I subscribed to the Government procurement website and several tenders were advertised and sent to my business email, which on the face of it were considered within my reach. However, for a start, they required experience, which was a challenge. Experience or a working skill is never a part of the best years of our learning scale 0-21 years old in our education system. Most students leave secondary and tertiary institutions without working experience or a skill. Sometimes, this forces many into depression and ultimately criminal activities, especially those who are forced into the burdensome trap of borrowing money and taking jobs that ensure they are unable to repay loans and live dignified lives at the same time.

Registration with the National Contracts Commission (NCC) was also a requirement for obtaining government contracts. I applied for said registration and was given the green light to register. However, I did not complete the registration, because the J$35,000 required then could not be paid within the prescribed time or at all. I was out of pocket. I eventually deregistered the business of AC&S Architects approximately 4 years later. Maybe I gave up too quickly. However, I would hasten to say, I have absolutely no regrets deregistering.

I applied to the National Housing Trust (NHT) and requested consideration for mortgage refinancing, as the rates offered were less than the credit union. However, they advised that it was against their policy to lend assistance since I had used up my NHT benefit when I bought the house. I had hoped that refinancing would be considered, given that I had paid off the NHT loan in short order. It seemed that I was stuck with the high interest rates at the Credit Union. I eventually sold the house and again another financial entity got most of the money. Both VMBS and the credit union made over $7 million in fake and real currency from the same house while I was left homeless. The couple who bought it would again be providing the NHT and the other mortgagor with millions more. I needed a drink at that point!!! Something strong to consume me!!! However, I easily settled for water.

Through it all, I remained passionate about living my best life ever and wished the same for all. I know it is very possible to live a dignified life, having a stable home and running water. This is a dream and is supposed to be a right, which can be realized by every human being.

PART 2: ECONOMIC SYSTEMS AND THEIR IMPACTS ON OUR LIVES

I became quite pensive about the economic systems that impact one's way of life and wondered about the different outcomes that would have been achieved in my situation, had the current systems been different. I compared a monetary run economic system with a collaborative work-based economic system and found I prefer the latter.

Here is a comparison of the monetary based economic system and the collaborative work-based economic system:

Monetary based economic system	Collaborative work-based economic system
1. Money based	1. Work based
2. Produces goods if money is available	2. Produces good without money
3. Values, prices, and sells based on weights	3. All are priceless and valuable, nothing to sell
4. People work for money	4. People work with purpose and pleasure
5. People work for money	5. People work to serve and be served
6. Money is limited in supply	6. No monetary limitations
7. Forced to borrow to survive	7. Survive without having to borrow
8. Receives little pay for hard work	8. Must work, multiple benefits from work
9. Rewards people lavishly for doing nothing	9. Must work, must be rewarded
10. Unstable and ripples multiple disasters	10. Stable and ripples multiply creativity
11. Presents in inflated languages	11. Presents in simple language and enlightens

12. Empowers people with money
12. Empowers all
13. Education for those with money
13. Education for all
14. Not all skill based
14. Inherently skill based
15. Specialized/limited skills
15. Multiple skills, no limitations
16. Monotonous
16. Promotes variety
17. Builds hostilities, wars, revenge
17. Embraces differences
18. Creates wealth for a few
18. Creates wealth for all
19. Gets rich producing bad products
19. No incentives for bad products
20. Gets rich from dishonesty
20. No incentives for dishonesty
21. Gets money for murder
21. No incentives for murder
22. Enslaves the majority
22. Gives responsible freedom for all
23. No guarantee of privacy
23. Privacy guaranteed
24. Inherently evil
24. Rooted in good but not immune to evil
25. Run by lies
25. Run by truth but not immune to lies
26. Creates product shortages and wastages
26. Creates products according to needs
27. Creates unmanageable greed
27. Greed is manageable
28. Based on inequality
28. Based on equality
29. Inherently corrupt
29. Inherently transparent but not immune
30. Creates inequity
30. Creates equity
31. Creates classism
31. Eliminates classism
32. Promotes competition
32. Promotes working together but not immune to competition
33. Creates widespread criminality
33. Not immune, may create a few criminals
34. Inherently corrupt
34. Inherently honest, but not immune to corruption
35. Inherently legalistic and unjust
35. Inherently legalistic but deals justly

36. Inherently tribal and divisive	36. Inclusive, not tribal, but not immune
37. Breeds multiple stresses	37. Eliminates most stressors
38. Breeds unhappiness and ill health	38. Breeds happiness and well being
39. Thrives on adversities and destruction	39. Builds to rid adversities and destructions
40. Robs family time	40. Promotes family time
41. Robs rest time	41. Promotes rest time
42. Health benefits for those with money	42. Health benefits for all
43. Works with very little to show	43. Works with plenty to show
44. No respect for the environment	44. Respect for the environment
45. Taxes, confines, and cripples diversity	45. Develops and expands
46. Guarantees death from unnatural causes	46. Die mostly from natural causes
47. Money disappears without a trace	47. No money to disappear
48. Every dollar counts	48. Every person counts

COLLABORATIVE WORK-BASED ECONOMY

A collaborative work-based economic system which requires all people to work without money, will reap approximately 90% success, both to preserve most of the Earth's natural resources and to promote health and wellness. When people contribute labor, knowing that the entire country they reside in requires their work, skills, and services to function effectively and efficiently, and in the same breath having their material needs met from said collective work, what could be a better incentive to work when you matter, and not money?

A work-based economic system essentially requires that all citizens should have the opportunity to engage in work, which is never in short supply. Currently however, the unemployment figure is astronomical and many including highly skilled individuals are unemployed due to lack of resources among potential employers. It is for this reason that a work- based economy aims to eliminate lack through continuous work while preventing burn-out through the implementation of a rotation system. God created work for the joy and health of all humankind. The essence of such an economic system is the preservation of the Earth which is necessary for man's survival; hence the principle of shared work to lessen the load is also applied. The wise man Solomon said that two are better than one because they have a good reward for their labor, because if one falls, the one will lift the other up. The benefits presented under the column of the work-based economic system clearly demonstrate this point. They also clearly show that a work-based economic system is the most effective approach in management to getting the best out of people who are created unique and diverse. Variety is indeed the spice of life.

A Monetary run Economic System

A monetary run economic system is used to govern all countries in the world where money is used to create work and to pay people for said work they perform. The huge catch is, there is never ever enough money or work available to the majority so they can indeed work and be paid. Hence, this is a neatly designed system of catch 22 and money hoax which has not bettered lives. The activities generated by using money to balance lives does the very opposite, creating endless imbalances destroying families and much of the Earth's natural resources due to a lack of said money, and greed. Individuals compete for the scarce benefits and spoils that are manmade tampering and destroying earth valuable resources in the process.

Policies under a monetary run economic system are unjust, self-serving and facilitate insanity. Utilizing this model produces more of the same as it is fueled by lack of work and lack of money, yet those in charge forever promise progress and prosperity amidst lack of work and money. What sheer hoax and utter madness.

In a monetary run economic system money is used as a tool to mobilize all work activities for the survival of citizens. In the same breath, those who are responsible for its creation and supply set up various systems of control that prevent its availability to mobilize works and services that are critical to the survival of citizens. In such an economy, both workers and those who do not work, especially the latter, can acquire large amounts of money, which will be reflected in lifestyles that conjure up emotions of suspicion, anxiety, and anger among those who toil endlessly and are not able to match or come close to such lifestyles. This includes the owning of expensive real estate and expensive motor vehicle assets by some who are not known or seen to hold jobs, while those hard at work are not even able to own a National Housing Trust house or an inexpensive motor car. It is also an economy that is sustained by perpetual loan, perpetual borrowing and perpetual lack of money, lack of knowledge, lack of food, lack of water, and everything that citizens need to live happy and fulfilling lives in a world of abundance.

WASTAGES UNDER A MONETARY BASED ECONOMIC SYSTEM

Throughout the world (including Jamaica), tons of food go to waste annually, while millions go hungry due to lack of money in the hands of the needy to purchase the very food that cost farmers money to plant, tend, and reap. For example, hundreds of oranges, chochos, onions, potatoes and many other vegetables, fruits and ground provision spoil daily in the marketplace when not purchased and consumed. Except for honey, there are spoilages of dry and processed foods as well, if not used before the assigned expiry date, while millions go hungry and some die from starvation just because they lack work to earn money to make purchases.

On many occasions, foods which have been purchased reveal traces of spoilage, causing consumers to dispose of parts or all, depending on the food item and the extent of the trace. Taking spoilt food back to the seller is oftentimes costlier than the price of the item, hence consumers suffer monetary losses which could amount to thousands of dollars. Under a monetary based system, one can expect constant waste and monetary losses while human beings suffer. Although some waste could be avoided by utilizing agro-processing to create by-products especially when there is an exceptionally good season for that product, it is not done on a wide scale because of the lack of money to facilitate the setting up of many processing centers island-wide. This is not so under a work-based economy. Not only will there be people with the requisite skills and talents to process the excess foods, but others will work to create the appropriate storage centers for very long shelf life for future use. Having excess produce under a work- based system will also be a deliberate act to allow us meaningful engagements with neighboring countries. We will exchange or sell to those who wish to exchange or buy, and then acquire products or commodities that we need and are not able to produce.

FOOD SAFETY

Food safety is compromised under a monetary run economy. Unscrupulous people often produce counterfeit food as they do money, exposing citizens to serious illnesses and death, all to earn big bucks. People steal and sell foods that have high exposure to dangerous chemicals, also to earn money. If potential buyers are alerted quickly, all that loot goes to waste. If not, another health hazard is forced upon citizens, all compliments of a monetary based economic system where people are primarily motivated by money and not service to fellowmen.

UTILITIES

When citizens cannot pay utility companies for the services of light and water, the services are disconnected. Many will in turn reconnect and use it free of cost. The utility companies will declare billions of dollars in losses annually from theft. Tell me about the group of people in Jamaica who will sit back, roll over and die from not having water in their pipes and electricity flowing through their cables? If they are unable to buy water and electricity; if they are unable to work to contribute to the production of clean water and electricity, they will simply steal it.

The aim of the collaborative work-based economic system is to utilize work to solve the problems that only work can solve. It has been said, "Don't be upset with the results you didn't get for the work you didn't do." People work, not money. Hence, people for example should be engaged according to their skill sets and talents to make the necessary piping and treatment connections carefully and intricately from the various safe and environmentally friendly water sources in the island to every home and public space that require the life-sustaining substance. In the same breath, a work-based economic system has a template which includes the need for rest, recreation, and healthy living.

Under the current system, money is required to engage in most recreational activities. Healthy living also requires money. Those without the necessary cash will not benefit from adopting healthy lifestyles and experiencing the therapeutic attributes of a variety of recreational activities. Collaborative and rotated work allow time off for rest for everyone. However, currently an individual will work at the same job for many years getting very little rest. The work is monotonous as one does the same thing repeatedly and the money earned is never enough to make a better life. No wonder, many who are not earning enough to take care of their basic needs will steal to do so. They will steal water, electricity, and just about everything that can be stolen. Is it not sad that one is unable to see the good in utilizing collaborative approaches in work and how it is indeed a recipe for the good life? This short-sightedness is unimaginable madness!

COMPROMISE'S HEALTH, FAMILY LIFE AND THE PLEASURES OF NATURE

Monetary run economies are a constant threat to having healthy populations and a healthy environment.

One set of persons will work themselves to death under a monetary based economic system, because paying the bills and buying food requires the money. They will work in sickness and 'til death do they part from around the office desk, to ensure an income. There are others who will not work yet they have a steady income.

Some time ago, I visited the office of a senior worker at the Heroes Circle National Insurance Scheme office. She was so sick that when I knocked on her office door, a faint answer to come in almost strained my ear. When I opened the door and entered, the desk was burdened with her upper body weight and she told me she was in pain. I collected the letter I went for, then went and got her some pain reliever and departed. This is an example of how under a monetary based system many will show up to work despite being sick just to earn an income. Multiply those times over.

Many workers also have very poor family life. Children yearn to have meaningful relationships with their parents who are often missing from their homes because they spend many hours at work slaving away for the dollars to provide for the material needs of the family. I am sure you constantly hear those hypocrites in the media playing experts as they expound on the rich benefits of family life to a country. They will tell you and rightly so that family comes first and many of our nation's children are not involved in family worship, they are not attending church, some attend school infrequently, many are undernourished, boys are negatively impacted finding more love and acceptance in criminal gangs over being loved by a father who is missing in action in the home, etc.

Although it is always said that it takes cash to care, it is mainly the lack of cash that divides families, as money is being chased to care for the material needs of the family. It takes work to earn the cash to care for the family. It is worse for a single parent home where there are three or more children to care for. Under a monetary-based economic system, how easy is it to provide for the material and physical needs of a family without money? There is also the scenario where a husband or a wife is always spending more time at work than with the family at home. The lonely wife or husband then finds an available partner. Look at how ridiculous this is. While many are slaving away, many are also idle. We have more than enough people with their mental faculties intact, who with a bit of training could relieve others from the stress of continuous work. That is work by rotation. This would not just allow all to participate in the dignity and value of contributing their time and talent to work but would also allow for quality family interactions in the homes, not to mention the blessings in spending time in God's beautiful scenes in nature that the removal of idle hands would facilitate.

Reach Falls in Portland is not just for those with money. A hike to the Blue Mountain should not just be a fleeting thought in the minds of many. Going to the beach or going fishing should not just be a dream for the majority. Traveling to all parishes in Jamaica and elsewhere outside of Jamaica should be within the reach of every single citizen of Jamaica. With people working and having free periods to spend in nature without the burden of not knowing the source of their next meal, there would be a considerable reduction in stress and by extension many illnesses.

I have heard complaints of being overworked and underpaid from nurses, teachers, factory workers and retail salespersons, employees within the police services and from many other work groups. These complaints are not unfounded. Many such workers suffer from various illnesses including hypertension, diabetes, obesity, stress, and mental illness.

Medical professionals say mental illness can be prevented. How? They say by holistic living. What is holistic living? Holistic living is when spiritual health, physical health, financial health, emotional health, and psychological health are positively promoted. This was endorsed in 2019 by a resident clinical psychologist in Montego Bay, Jamaica, on Healthy and Happy, a program aired on NCU Radio located in Mandeville. She disclosed that one out of four Jamaicans will experience mental illness. I believe the driving force behind this is the negative impact of a monetary based economic system, which demands the use of currencies for survival. Possession of currencies requires work and work is always either scarce or the income from work is inadequate.

The reality under such economic system is that financial health tops the list on the chart of holistic living. Although financial health is not entirely a guarantee for holistic living, it is nonetheless the primary facilitator. How is this so? Wholesome foods, water, relatively clean air, and shelter from the harsh elements in nature all requires money. Without employment and/or a reliable and consistent supply of money, holistic living for all Jamaicans will continue to remain a figment of one's imagination. In other words, money is silent weapon of mass destruction. Without the so-called money, one will not be able to purchase the essential foods, minerals and vitamins required for healthy living and will therefore become a candidate for all manner of illness.

Healthy foods promote physical health. However, healthy, and nourishing foods cost lots of money. If one wishes to farm healthy food, one will first need money to buy arable land, secure it, set up irrigation systems and such the like. So, cash is needed to experience physical health. Relatively clean air, potable water, sunshine, exercise, and rest promote psychological or mental health. When one's mental faculties are intact, spiritual health is enhanced. This will result in a healthy home environment, which maximizes emotional health and holistic living for all.

Real work encapsulates physical activity which strengthens the whole being. Exercise, relatively clean air, emotional wellbeing, mental health, and wellness are realized by doing real work. One must actively engage in physical labor to farm. Healthy and wholesome foods are produced from farming the land, and every human being must eat food to survive. Every human being should therefore at the very least play a role in the food industry whether by helping to plant, reap, process, test, distribute, etc. It is real work that provides reliable, consistent, and immediate access to water and everyone must consume water to survive. Therefore, every human being should also play a role in the production of potable water.

Real work produces sustainable shelters or homes for mankind. Real and rotative work guarantees rest and family time, which provides both physical and spiritual sunshine for all. Jesus promoted holistic living emphasizing physical health in his sojourn on Earth 2,000 years ago. He healed every form of sickness making individuals well to perform real work. In fact, 6,000 years ago, the Creator designed holistic living when he created Earth containing everything to support and sustain all life forms, no money included. Work was and remains the only force to sustain the environment thereby sustaining people. Satan and his Earthly representatives created the monetary economic system creating lacks, confusion, disorder, and every man for himself.

Every man who wants money to support himself and his family will indiscriminately take whatever he thinks is best for himself to put food on his table. He will cut trees from anywhere whether to burn coal or process lumber to sell. He will over fish and rape the seas of corals to sell. He will not care about maintaining fish sanctuaries. He will not care about protecting his environment from the onslaughts of disasters that his indiscriminate uses have exposed the nation to. He will burn tires at Riverton dump with no thought for the environment or the health of his neighbors, just to get the wires to sell. He will dump his garbage anywhere just to be rid of it, especially when the state is always failing to have trucks to collect it. He will not use his food money to pay a private carrier to dispose of his garbage. The easy way out is to dump it in the nearest gully with no care about possible flooding. He does not care if his actions will increase the rat or mosquito population. He reasons, it will in turn get him work to clean the gully so he can earn money.

He will overload his truck with quarry material, destroying the road to earn more money. He will use any waterfront property he can to engage in whatever business he deems will generate the most money and get away with this. He will build houses anywhere he can, to sell to make money and get away with it. There is no care that using Jamaican farmlands to build houses is a threat to being able to feed the nation. I guess that those in charge are happy for the opportunities it provides to their financial partners to import food which helps to cement their stronghold on food supplies. There is no doubt that controlling food supplies is tantamount to control over people's lives. We all must eat food to survive. There is also no care for the possible health hazard to the people as they become exposed to rejected foods and counterfeit products that are imported from time to time. Weak, feeble, and unhealthy people cannot sustain a strong healthy environment. These are the challenges presented under a monetary run economic system that promotes sheer individualism.

A monetary system generates sustained violence and criminality Because the monetary resource is always scarce, one must engage in competition for the little that is available to survive. A man will kill for as little as $50 to buy a bulla. It is said that a hungry man is an angry man. That is a fact. Robberies of cash and kind abound, as people try to get money or material to convert to money to survive. Billions of dollars will be stolen from public entities, and murderers will then be paid money to take out people who are a threat to uncover such robberies from the public purse. People will falsify documents to get jobs just to earn money. They will falsify documents or purchase counterfeit documents to travel overseas to what they hope will be a better life to earn cash. The better life can be had right here in Jamaica or anywhere else without money.

Money is the greatest obstacle to progress and prosperity. Several years ago, a Jamaican prime minister said, "We need to convert inner cities to winner cities." That can only be accomplished by using money in a monetary based economic system. I guess we will never have winner cities but forever inner cities. Where is the money to do this conversion? This is shear money hoax and hopelessness for most Jamaicans.

PROSTITUTION IS SUSTAINED IN A MONETARY BASED ECONOMIC SYSTEM

Prostitutes, mostly women engage in illicit sex with men, primarily to earn money. I see them every day. Those who are street prostitutes operate at nights. They smoke hard, quarrel a lot and stroll naked or half-naked up and down the streets to attract as many men as they can each night. One early morning I was stunned by the loud cries of one woman of the night. She was crying as she was robbed of her entire night's earning. On hearing her cries, I was almost moved to tears myself. I wished that I had some money to give her. It could be that she needed the money to pay the school fee to send her fatherless children to school, to pay her rent or mortgage or whatever.

If there are prostitutes under a work-based economic system, I guess they would prostitute for the fun of sex, to procreate, and to have responsible men as fathers. None would need to prostitute for school tuition, to pay rent, mortgage, utility bills, or to buy food, clothes or a house. What do you think? What do you think men would do if there were no prostitutes on the streets at nights? Do you think some women were born to become prostitutes? Do you have family members who are prostitutes?

LIVING WITHIN ONE'S MEANS

I find it quite amusing, that under a monetary based economic system, people are repeatedly told to live within their means. They are further told that living within their means will guarantee them less stressful lives and by extension, it will be better for the overall economy. They have even scolded the Government of Jamaica for borrowing too much. This is laughable madness, a complete lie, and totally impossible under a monetary based economic system.

Living within one's means is being able to use one's income to take care of one's needs without having to borrow. However, on the contrary and in the same breath, people are encouraged to borrow money, which is to live above one's means. One must be fast asleep not to be aware of the numerous advertisements and teasers in the media by lending institutions, luring citizens to borrow money at low interest rates. In fact, to further capture people's attention and get them trapped into indebtedness, institutions persuade them to borrow and use other people's money to improve their lives. Does it make sense that while being encouraged to reduce your indebtedness and refrain from borrowing you are also being encouraged to make use of low interest loans that are available in the marketplace? Could it be that a monetary run economy cannot function without loans? It sure cannot; in fact, loans are the engines that drive such an economy. Government therefore loves borrowing too. They will always borrow, and squander cash and citizens will have to repay.

What would be the impact on said economy if all were to live within their means, and those with loans settle their debts immediately? Obviously, the monetary economy would simply go into shock. The banking or financial sector could no longer negotiate loans to expand the money pool. This would affect manufacturing and all other critical sectors. If no one is borrowing, no new money will be created to make the rounds into the hands of thousands of people for them to spend. If people are not spending, products will not sell and therefore production must decrease. This leads to job cuts. Loss of jobs means loss of income, which would lead to stagflation and a chaotic society. Notwithstanding, the society is chaotic under a monetary based economic system because there are still job cuts, loan defaults, crime and violence as people steal and kill to get money for their survival.

This is the worst part. Under a monetary based system there are no laws that compel people to work to acquire money. Therefore, those without jobs must acquire money via other means to survive. These other means such as stealing, begging, inheriting, and finding create vibrancy in every so-called functional economy. These monies must keep changing hands for the monetary based system to function. So, having acquired it by whatever means necessary, one is then forced to use it to purchase goods and services to stay alive.

Needing money to live or to survive, often branded as, "it takes cash to care", is a lie that minds have been programmed to accept as the ideal model to manage economic affairs, labor, people, and the world at large.

People do not and cannot live within their means under a monetary based economic system. Their need for food, water, clothes, household furniture, appliances, houses, and cars must be met; hence they are compelled to acquire these commodities. They will utilize any and every conceivable method to do so because they cannot live or function without them.

Everyone does not possess the wherewithal to produce all that is needed for survival. Therefore, those who qualify will engage with money lending corporations for a loan to purchase any goods or services their income would not allow them to acquire. Sellers of monetary loans are ready and always on hand to help. They are aware that most workers have very little disposable income. This awareness is key in the design of the monetary based system. It must be noted too that those who do not qualify for loans, will engage other means to acquire money to satisfy their material needs.

Therefore, borrowing money is essentially having to live above one's means when one's salary is always never enough to satisfy such needs. This dilemma obtains in Jamaica and the rest of the world. Moreover, as you borrow, you become a slave to the lender.

Despite public outcry for citizens and governments to live within their means, the arguments presented above show they simply cannot and will not live within means. It is totally impossible to do so under a monetary based economy. Citizens are therefore forced to acquire and use money to purchase goods and services required for survival.

Perpetual spending translates to perpetual indebtedness and perpetual stress. This ensures perpetual consumption, which ensures continuous movement of money from banks to banks and hands to hands.

However, there is constant disequilibrium and gaps in this model, because spending and consuming patterns vary, further resulting in many disasters with multiple ripples. This difficulty in judging and predicting patterns of consumption creates cycles of anxiety, fear, worry and uncertainty. These are known stresses that thrive on the calamity called lack; lack of knowledge, lack of education and lack of money to pay.

Because survival is the strongest desire for every human, the desire, and the will to pay and survive will play out at all costs. At all costs includes and is not limited to stealing money to buy the furniture, selling illegal drugs to pay the mortgage or rent, stealing electricity, stealing water, scamming, prostitution, murder, compromises on health as in the buying of less healthy foods to afford paying school fees, resorting to unhealthy habits such as smoking to relieve stress, getting another job with the ripple effect of spending less time with family especially children, hiding from loan companies, and the list goes on and on. For some it is their sole desire to capture more money to lift one's living standard even amid wallowing in miseries through it all and creating a multiplicity of other miseries.

In a collaborative work-based economic system, survival of all people forms the essence. Working is the key for survival and not money hence the people's survival is hinged to work. In fact, everything that money is used to buy can only be made available by WORK. Work is therefore engaged to satisfy people's need for food, water, homes, transportation, furniture, education, multiple skills and more. People are encouraged to work according to their life's purpose manifested in a corresponding set of skills developed over time through a collaborative approach. The approach is rooted in an acceptance that the world of resources is owned by all, and through discovering and learning from nature, sharing, and teaching, the resources are utilized responsibly through work for the good of all, and the good of the Earth in a perpetual partnership of sustenance. The likelihood of people becoming stressed is at a low because the collective labor and the opportunity to rotate labor, allow off time for people to both rest and recreate and produce enough of the most basic of resources for all, such as healthy foods, reliable water supply, clothes and homes designed to decent standards. People will therefore benefit from excellent health of mind, body, and spirit. By adapting a collaborative approach to labor our innate programming for happiness, gratitude, humility, love, kindness, gentleness, meekness, compassion, honesty, beauty, justice, joy, peace, empathy, service, faith, hope and truth will be stimulated and manifested in our attitudes towards fellowman.

In a monetary based economic system, money is the key to survival. Most people who earn money from working in such an economy are often not able to purchase many other things they need to survive after spending on basic needs such as food, utilities, clothes, and education for children. They have limited cash to acquire a skill, purchase a house, a car, new household furniture or new appliances, which are usually costly. Therefore, they borrow, and with the requirement to pay back with interest added to the principal borrowed, they default on the loans; some temporarily, others for many years. The reasons for breakdowns in repayments are many and varied. Some defaults are due to illnesses, death, price increases in consumables but no corresponding salary increase and loss of jobs which unavoidably lead to stress. Stress is a definite trigger for many societal ills such as anger, lying, false pride, resentment, arrogance, egoism, envy, bad mind, greed, and feelings of being inferior. So, because of stress from the lack of money to purchase necessities to survive, evil tendencies are manifested to counter such injustice and is manifested in anger, resentment, lies, greed, murder, false pride, envy, bad mind, inferiority complex, egoism, arrogance, etc.

SEVEN WAYS MONEY GETS IN THE HAND

To date, I have discovered that there are seven (7) ways to get money in hand. They are as follows:

Work for it or being employed

Borrow it from an institution or individual

Charge it/tax it or create a fee for anything you can

Inherit it/being born into wealth or dead left' or receiving settlement from insurance claims

Find it

Beg it, such as individual or institutionalized begging or gamble to win it

Steal it/corruption/drug deals/extortions/break-ins/scamming, etc.

I am of the belief that being employed or having a job to earn, is everyone's initial dream under a monetary based economic system, until at some point in a person's life the dream is either realized or lost, because the monetary system is indeed a hoax.

People have been told that one ought to work for money. However, in the same breath work is in short supply. People are also criticized as being unfair in their work relationship with each other because they charge excessively for both excellent and mediocre work. Some will also collect incomes for work not done and I know you can add to the list.

Someone once declared that there can never be fairness under a monetary run economy. How do people balance their financial lives working for an income, which is not able to meet their greater need for food, water, energy, housing, healthcare, and emergencies without which their survival is at risk? Their needs collectively exceed their incomes month after month, year after year. How can people be expected to display humane behavior to each other when the pressures of work to earn a living does not equate to work as an act of service to one's fellowman?

WORK FOR IT/BORROW IT

Work for it and borrow it are the first two items on the money acquisition list. These have been paired because they are unavoidably interrelated. One without the other cancels both and here is how. When you are working and getting paid in monetary terms, it is easy for an individual or an institution to trust you with a loan. If you have a very good idea backed by a well written business plan you may also get a loan although it has become very unlikely in these times.

All institutionalized loans require at the top of the list of criteria, proof of income. To borrow from an individual without knowing where the funds will originate to repay can prove very dangerous. You need a form of income stream to repay any loan.

Lack of work under a monetary run economy is extremely popular. So, with "work for it" and "borrow it" cancelled, this now leaves an individual at very high risk not just to oneself but to the wider society.

With many people unable to find employment today coupled with those employed being underpaid, is it any surprise there is a prevalence in all the other areas of the monetary acquisition list, where stealing, and charge it/tax it tops the list?

Charge it/Tax it

Third on the list (charge it/tax it) is a first cousin to number seven (steal it) but it is still able to stand firm on its own. Governments first come to mind, as income tax, education tax, property tax, general consumption tax and other taxes are taken from citizens. Motor vehicle insurance is also a tax levied on the owners of motor vehicles.

It is also quite common to see men position themselves in both public and private car parks throughout the country and charge motor vehicle operators a parking fee. Whether you spotted the vacant space in a public parking lot or was shown by the men who place themselves on location, you are expected on your return to your vehicle to pay a tax for the unsolicited safe keeping of your vehicle. Would one consider such to be work? Ah well, creative self-employment could be used to describe such activities. Imagine what it would be like if all the unemployed were to enter this type of trade?

Creative self-employment is also at work when one is led without requesting a guide to a public/private transportation which you must take to journey home, and the guide who is also called a loader man taxes your driver.

Another example of "charge it" is a scenario in which some schools were charging students to sit a Grade 4 mock literacy test. What are the questions to ponder regarding the scenario? Did the education ministry lack the money to pay for proper administration of the test or did they refused to pay although they had the money? How many times do people have money to spend but delay or refuse to spend because if they spend it to pay for an exam, they will either go hungry for weeks, have their electricity disconnected or be in problems with the landlord or mortgage company?

Therefore, if money is always in short supply, what is so wrong with the teachers using one of the seven ways to get money, which is to tax the students for sitting an examination that costs? And catch 22 comes into play because Money HOAX is like being between a rock and a hard place.

Without money, the education system, the health system, the road networks, the agricultural sector and just about every critical and essential service in every country will be compromised. The case of the Victoria Jubilee Hospital (for maternity patients) being without essential elevator services for seven months is a perfect example of such compromises.

Charge it/tax it is the government's main source of income coupled with borrowing from the owners of money to fund all services. Money simply cannot be created without loans.

Therefore, if governments proclaim that money is always in short supply, work will also always be in short supply, and if money is required to pay for just about every essential service, then a great majority of people will not be able to benefit from these essential services. As such, the parents or students should simply pay to take the test if they are lucky to have the cash, or not take the test if they cannot pay.

Charge it/tax it, is the second most widely used money acquisition monopoly in all human affairs. "And it came to pass in those days, that there went out a decree from Caesar Augustus, that all the world should be taxed" (Luke 2:1).

All motorists are required to pay motor vehicle insurance to insurance companies to use the public road network legally. This pooled fee is charged annually and is justified against the background that if you were to have a road accident you would be protected against the risks associated with motor vehicle accidents. If, however, you do not have an accident, you cannot make a claim on the insurance company for a fee refund.

You are required to keep paying for as long as you own a functional motor vehicle and use the roads. You will only benefit from these pooled funds if you have an accident and make a valid claim. Some insured persons retire from driving or die without having an accident or making a claim. Others have accidents and some even die by driving recklessly whether by speeding or being under the influence of alcohol. Accident survivors may or may not be compensated for their loss by insurance companies as settlement of claims depend on what can be proven. It can be a most unusual win/lose situation and therefore I am of the strong opinion that motor vehicle insurance is a most complicated type of monetary acquisition. It is indeed a charge or tax akin to gambling that is administered by force.

The insurance scheme simply boils down to people continuously pooling money for the purpose of being able to claim against the risks associated with motor vehicle collisions and the probability is that some will have accidents while the majority will not. Invariably, the majority will not benefit from pooled funds. Many will also be frustrated when the claims fall woefully short in relieving them of the financial burden from accidents in which the vehicle was written off, and then out of necessity, they must engage with a financial entity for a new loan to purchase another vehicle.

Some years ago, I was about four to six months away from completely repaying my car loan. Another motorist broke a stop sign and hit my car. Before the accident, the car was in excellent driving condition with many more years to offer. It was extensively damaged and had to be written off. I was severely setback for several months, as I had to travel by bus and taxi sometimes to stay afloat and generate an income to care for my child and myself. Those were miserable days. The cash I eventually got from his insurance company was not enough for me to purchase a similar reliable car. My insurance company paid me not a dollar. Totally disappointed and with a very heavy heart, I had to borrow again to purchase another reliable car with three new long years to repay, when I should have rid myself of indebtedness in less than six months. I literally hate loans. They are most stressful and fortunately, I also hate stress, especially stress that is brought on by fake loans.

Those who are unlucky to have an accident and can receive cash from making a claim will benefit or hit a small part of the insurance jackpot just from having contributed to the pool.

If someone dies from the accident, it is a win/lose scenario, as the life cannot be returned to the corpse with money that may be derived from a claim by someone else. If the accident did not involve another motor vehicle but only caused damages to a tree or stone by the roadside, such might be a win for the insurance company, with nothing or very little to pay out if the insured chose to make a claim. Those who are lucky not to have an accident cannot make a claim and will not benefit from having contributed to the pool of funds. They will simply lose their money.

In February 2015 several parliamentarians in the Government of Jamaica voiced their support to seize any motor vehicle being driven on the road without being legally insured. In fact, any motor vehicle owner driving without insurance would have to pay large fines. I have decided to analyze and to put further thought to the government's declaration to make this into law, after listening to the following interview.

On February 19, 2015 the hosts of the Jamaican morning talk show program Fresh Start on Newstalk 93FM engaged Dr. Parris Lyew-Ayee, Director of Mona Geo-Informatics Institute, on his research findings on road traffic accidents in Jamaica. His data showed that number one on the list of road traffic accidents involved pedestrians. He stated that the very pedestrians themselves cause most of these accidents which result in deaths and injuries. I am yet to see the pedestrian "walk-foot" insurance. Please don't get any ideas now to implement one.

A distant second on his list is reckless driving and speeding motorists who believe they own the roads and are oftentimes seen switching from lane to lane in violation of the legal space of other drivers.

The matter of road infrastructure was discussed against the background given by Dr. Parris Lyew-Ayee that a road is not made for pedestrians to cross. Therefore, sidewalks, bridges, pedestrian crossings are critical interventions to assist in the safety of both pedestrians and motorists alike. Dr. Lyew-Ayee used the data given to him by the police and stated that even where sidewalks and pedestrian crossings are in place pedestrians are so suicidal that they insist on remaining in the roadway causing deaths and injuries. He did not and no doubt could not present data to say whether it was the reckless and speeding drivers, who collided with the reckless, suicidal, and careless pedestrians. It could make sense that insurance companies should therefore not be concerned about paying out claims for injuries and deaths caused by suicidal behaviors once proven.

Is suicide tendency ever taken into consideration when investigating motor vehicle accidents involving pedestrians?

Let's consider another side of the coin where concerted efforts are made on the part of road safety entities, the police, the government and of course the rest of us who are not suicidal and reckless, to prevent motor vehicle accidents. As people respond positively to such appeals the likelihood of motor vehicle accidents may decrease. This effort becomes very important against the background that every year to sensitize citizens, the media broadcast the number of deaths from road accidents.

Dr. Parris Lyew-Ayee also informed that cameras are installed on the roads in some countries to identify traffic violations, and this leads to offenders being ticketed and fined. Since then, Jamaica has made progress in installing cameras at the expense of its citizens for this purpose.

Motorists under the watchful eyes of cameras and the police, will be ticketed and fined for traffic offences. In the same breath they are continuously being charged motor vehicle insurance as a safeguard in the event of an accident. The government benefits by earning additional revenue as more traffic offenders are caught by the police who are also paid from the taxes collected from said citizens. The insurance companies also collect more premiums as drivers try harder to avoid driving without insurance. The insurance companies also look forward to having fewer claims to pay out as more customers drive more carefully to avoid accidents.

Why are we all forced to invest in an insurance pool where many are guaranteed to lose cash times over? Similarly, why is it that the government is considering amendment of the Road Traffic Act to seize vehicles if owners are found not to have invested in the gambling pool? Charge it or tax it is clearly at work. Charge it/tax it favors corporations and their employees. It is their main source of income. Under a monetary based economic system, adversities are always opportunities; hence perpetual adversities must be created.

So, clearly charge it/tax it is highly favored by governments to boost revenues, pay themselves and finance interests from loans. Why loans? Because borrowing is the lifestyle of governments. It is what they do best. Who do they borrow from? Where did such money come from to lend? Who worked to manufacture it? Who pays for its manufacturing? Where did the material come from to make the money? Who mined the material to manufacture the money?

Governments' work is talk, borrow money for everything, travel the world, meet their counterparts at summits and world conferences, make oppressive laws to create perpetual poverty and other laws favoring a rich minority that continues to rule the poor majority, tax the people, and earn wages from such fake work.

INHERIT IT

To inherit money can at times be a sad occasion. Nevertheless, it can be a happy one too if there is immediate cash to pass on to the surviving relative. Governments are big beneficiaries of dead-lef properties that were not bequeathed, as well as those willed to surviving relatives. Lawyers and governments benefit from fees resulting from the process of administration and probates of wills. However, this process can take years to complete causing frustration for surviving family members. Some will die before the process is completed. Monetary inheritance cannot be relied on as a good source of income. However, it is always a reliable source of income for governments and attorneys.

FIND IT

Finders' keepers could be a reliable source of income, only if people were throwing away thousands of dollars on the streets, or if they were finding ganja and cocaine at sea regularly and were able to convert these to cash. They are not. Ganja and cocaine are illegal drugs. Money found in an amount below one hundred thousand dollars will not be of any great help to anyone who does not have a mindset for prudence in investing. Are you one who can invest a reasonable amount of cash in a business, roll it over and produce profit enough to develop an income stream from it? How many persons to date have found up to one hundred thousand dollars in the streets and have been able to create financial wealth? Find it is not an answer.

BEG IT

Beggars on the other hand have fared much better than finders of cash. Some localized beggars are quite content to be able to eat a food daily for many years while also developing a savings plan, which assist with other needs. However, institutionalized beggars are quite the professionals. They can avoid tax it as they set up foundations and road races and they are quite wealthy. They distribute food, medical equipment, houses, clothing, furniture, scholarships, etc. If you have the expertise this could become a reliable income source. I hope to set up a foundation account and distribute cash only.

Gamble and win it cannot stand on its own and although appended to beg it, it can be appended to all other ways to acquire money. Anyone with money can gamble and hopefully win additional money.

Thief it

How many persons are thieves? Would you consider yourself a thief? Mankind places a monetary value on almost everything that is required for surviving in this world except the air we breathe. Therefore, surviving could be likened to money earned or stolen. Have you ever picked a mango or an apple from any property not registered as yours? If so, you would have stolen mangoes or apples, which is stealing money. Is steal it a better option than find it?

Money is tied to your life or to your survival and you are required to work to earn money to live although you are not compelled in law to work Nonetheless, work is scarce, and I am also very aware that many do not work yet earn money in abundance. However, if you are not able to work to earn money which would eliminate borrowing it, then you would need to utilize one or several of the five remaining options. They are beg it, find it, inherit it, charge it/tax it or steal it. Perhaps being lazy could be added as another option to acquiring money from the mere fact that many acquire cash without having to work at all. Which do you use to acquire money?

To date, steal it, borrow it, beg it and charge it/tax it seems to be the most utilized options in acquiring money. For as long as the gain from work is money and for as long as a huge majority of the Earth's people remains unemployed, steal it, charge it/tax it and beg it will be the main methods used in the acquisition of money. Yet many are devious hypocrites as they will have available employment or work to be done but will not employ you as they claim they have no money to pay you while those in their employ will be overworked and paid meager wages. They are also very good at devising schemes to underpay or not to pay agreed amounts. Interestingly, they will be the first to criticize the beggar and condemn those who steal money or food suggesting they be locked away, and they are also very quick to rejoice when the man who steals a goat is beaten to death by a mob who are themselves thieves.

IS THE ACCUMULATION OF BANKS OF MONEY A MARK OF SUCCESS?

On Tuesday February 17, 2015, Member of Parliament for South Central St. Catherine, Dr. Andrew Wheatley, made the following statement on Fresh Start, a Jamaican morning talk show program. He said that from his years of experience in politics, he realized that people are driven in life because of money.

Is it money that drives you to survive in this life? Is it money that drives you to work? Is it money that drives you to succeed at your job? Is it money that drives people to steal money from others? Some steal not just from the living but from the dead. Is it money that drives the doctor to learn and excel in the field of medicine, to make accurate diagnoses and administer the appropriate treatments for the health and wellbeing of the patient, or is the doctor driven by his desire to serve? Would you describe the health and wellness of the patient as success or does the doctor's ability to serve equals success, or is it both?

Does it mean that success is to accumulate, understand, interpret, and administer knowledge in service to mankind or does it mean that success is the accumulation of millions of dollars having served mankind? "Success is knowing your purpose in life, growing to reach your maximum potential, and sowing seeds that benefit others." - John C. Maxwell

Is it not absurd to think that one's success in life is hinged on money? Is it that money is more important than human development? Does that make sense?

Which comes first: you, knowledge, money, success, or work? Is it possible that without money one cannot accumulate, understand, and interpret knowledge in service to mankind? How important is it to accumulate, understand and interpret knowledge in service to mankind? Do these actions evoke emotions of love, joy, happiness, excitement, or is it money that evokes such emotions?

How important is love, joy, happiness, and excitement to you? Is it love, joy, happiness, and excitement that drive your success or is it money that drives you to love, be joyful, happy, excited, and successful?

Is the doctor able to achieve success because of his own independent actions? Is it accurate to say the doctor's success was made possible by money, or was it due to other factors? Clearly, it could not be money so what brought about his success? Could it be two human beings moved by their need for each other?

So, the doctor would have attained knowledge in medicine. The patient presents an illness, and the doctor uses the wisdom, knowledge and understanding to administer the appropriate treatment. The patient recovers and is again healthy. Hence, both human beings reached out to each other to solve a problem. Did money bestow the doctor's understanding of medicine to diagnose and treat the illness presented?

What do we know about knowledge, interpreting, understanding, and administering treatment and care? It seems to me that they all came from a human source and required human input. In fact, all wisdom, knowledge, and understanding come from God. It is God who puts knowledge in mankind's heart to teach each other without any form of monetary exchange. In Exodus 35:30-36 we are told that it is God who fills us with his spirit in wisdom, knowledge and understanding and in all manner of workmanship and has put in our hearts to teach.

It is obvious that without the patient and the doctor to serve, all other factors seemed meaningless. It is also quite compelling that the patient contributed to the doctor's success and vice versa. Is this the reason there is no "I" in success? It appears so, because without the "U" the other letters make no sense. Again, let us not leave money out of the picture. Unfortunately, there is no "U" or "I" in Money.

So, what part did money play? Would money be of any use without the patient? Would money be of any use without the doctor? Did the money drive the doctor to serve and treat the patient? Did the money drive the patient to see and serve the doctor? Would it be difficult to conclude that success is about service to each other and not money? In other words, we all must serve each other for success to occur. Is that not a satisfying experience? Furthermore, whether money exists or not, humans have needs requiring human touch and correspondingly humans have the knowledge, the hands, hearts, and the resourceful Earth to satisfy the corresponding needs.

But, in our world today why is money the mark of success and not service to each other? Do you know why?

The doctor is compensated handsomely for serving the patient. Did we just conclude that success occurs when we serve each other? Is the patient compensated for serving the doctor? Why not? Without the patient, there is no success for the doctor; if there is no sickness, a doctor is of no use. Why not pay the patient some money too? Why is it important to compensate the doctor and not the patient? The patient served the doctor, and the doctor served the patient correspondingly. The doctor gets money in addition to being served and so should the patient in addition to serving the doctor. Is the scale balanced? Plain and simple, it is money hoax.

In fact, why do we really need compensation at all? If I serve you and you serve me, does that not nullify monetary compensation as the service each receives satisfies both needs? Is that not where the value lies? Or is it that the value lies only in money?

"The meaning of life is to find your gift. The purpose of life is to give it away." - Pablo Picasso

"But whoso hath this world good, and seeth his brother has need and shutteth up his bowel of compassion from him, how dwelleth the love of God in him?" (1 John 3:17).

Seeing then that money is tied to life on Earth, may we get more of it from those who have lots of it to improve our Earthly lives? Is there any interest in using money to improve lives or is it simply a part of a plan to use it as a tool to manipulate and control lives?

PART 3: COMPETITION THE HUGE EVIL

Competition is an enemy to unity in diversity, hence competition is an enemy to common good, common sense and common values. Competition eliminates, separates, divides and is a huge evil. "The End Game of Competition is Monopoly."

Competition as the name implies is one competing against another to win, which means the other loses. Invariably, whoever wins is famed or crowned. The winner takes the prize, receives the coveted endorsements, and will do whatever it takes to remain the winner for as long as possible. It is the dream of many to attain such position of stronghold. Some realize the dream; others keep dreaming and still others lose hope.

According to world standards, competition runs the world. What a world! Countries compete, governments compete, people compete, and the winner takes all. It is referenced as the game where the fittest of the fit survive. The winner is constantly seen as a spectacle to be coveted, competed against, and dethroned. This is war in perpetuity.

In the game, some will win today, lose tomorrow, some just keep losing. Some are accidentally hurt in the process of competing, others by a deliberate act of inflicting hurt and pain on others, some maimed, some die, and others are pleasured by it all win or lose.

All governments and their supporting corporations encourage and endorses competition among their citizenry from the womb to the tomb. However, all governments are winners. They assume all power and ownership of all resources and monopolize citizens to compete. Most countries with the backings of their supporting monetary corporations run a two-party game of monopolizing citizens. One party in today, the other four to five years after but the monopoly does not change. It remains one or the other party against citizens. What a game! The coveted prize is wealth, power, and manipulation of resources, which includes people.

Wealth and power are key. Ordinary eyes are not able to understand the construct of the seat of such power and wealth. Status, power, and money translate to control and manipulation of others by the holders of such. Proverbs 22:7 says, "The rich ruleth over the poor, and the borrower is servant to the lender".

Former American president, James Garfield stated, "Whoever controls the volume of money in our country is absolute master of all industry and commerce and when you realize that the system is very easily controlled one way or another by a few powerful men at the top, you will not have to be told how periods of inflation and depression originate."

Those without money or education are at times referred to as losers and lazy. They are totally oblivious to the fact that losers and laziness are inherent in the system. Losing, failing, winning, being eliminated or elevated, being left behind, illiteracy, are key players in the systems of governing in a world of competition. Policies are crafted to ensure that poverty, illiteracy, and joblessness reign. Competition is not fair. It cannot be fair. Everyone is different.

Those who craft such policies are very entertained by sufferings. If you do not believe me, check this out. "Single acts of tyranny may be ascribed to the accidental opinion of the day; but a series of oppressions, begun at a distinguished period, and pursued unalterably through every change of administration too plainly proves a deliberate, systematic plan of reducing us to slavery." - Thomas Jefferson

Check this out too. Are you a boxing fan? Many boxing fans find pleasure in seeing their favorite boxer hitting the daylight out of his opponent. They cheer at the sight of blood running, huge swelling over the very delicate and tender eyes, and the sight of a knockout punch sending a body hitting hard on the ground. They clap and cheer. There are many other violent sports, which attract many people who hit the roof with glee at the downfall of an entire team. Governments share the same glee at the misery of the people they govern. The people cannot help but do the same. "It is no measure of health to be well adjusted to a profoundly sick society." - Jiddu Krishnamurti

The system through competition assigns the labels of losers, failures, and poor people to its citizens. Losers become outcasts and are further labeled covetous, bad minded, thieves and a threat to those who have.

Sadly, by the very competing act, they become a threat to others like themselves who also have very little. They compete and the fittest survive the competition for scarce benefits and spoils as mayhem and death result. Proverbs 28:3 says, "A poor man that oppresseth the poor is like a sweeping rain which leaveth no food."

Oftentimes an athlete who keeps losing in sports resorts to cheating to get in the limelight and to acquire the winning status. Because competition is fierce and requires a winner, the fierce competitors will use performance- enhancing drugs, match fixing, or excessive violence and intimidation in sports. As always, those who do, hope never to be caught. Sometimes they enjoy years of fame and status before being caught.

Businesses that have attained status via competition always use their financial strength to do all that it takes to retain or maintain such leading status for as long as they are able to do so. Others are always competing to uproot them for the status.

A reporter in Kolkata, India, explained that competition must be fierce as it is all about survival. This fierceness is not to be taken lightly as ultimately you are overtaken by it and don't even know it; your life is no longer your own and you don't even know it. It is for this reason that children are groomed for the world of competing and they live what they learn. Do you understand why our children and young adults fight to overthrow each other and harm, hurt and kill the way they do for money and power?

A top food processing company will have all eyes and ears on the ground in the marketplace to ensure they acquire or eliminate any new idea that could threaten their leading status. That is how some companies become authority businesses. Instead of 50 companies, which would mean more variety, more employment, and of course more products, you have only 20, which means more scarcities in many areas and therefore very high prices and huge profits.

Bear in mind that huge profits oftentimes mean profits to probably 10 from those 20 companies. The other 10 may have marginal profits and are struggling because there is still fierce competition with 4-6 from the lot wanting to be the only companies to make the product as everyone would have to buy from them and they would assume awesome power, becoming dictators.

Of course, they would also among themselves behind closed doors, agree to monopolize the marketplace while giving the impression that competition is the greatest thing. They tell you that competition is good but believe me they HATE competition.

According to the famous financial mogul John D. Rockefeller, "Competition is a sin." He knew very well that it was a sin when he suffered losses against his competitor, hence he collaborated and joined forces with his competitor and benefited greatly. It is said that many used competitions to shrink and drive many financial institutions out of business causing many job losses, loss of money and hardships on many people many decades ago, and it continues today. Is competition fair?

When Trinidad and Tobago can 'defy the odds' and get other Caribbean islands to purchase as much of their produce as they can get them to buy, this is called competition. Filling up other shops and stores with their products means more sales for them and perhaps more employment for Trinidadians. Trinidad wins, the other islands lose.

Why do the losers then rant and rave and even appeal for boycott of products from Trinidad and Tobago when competition is such a good thing? If you say something is so good and healthy why holler and bawl when you lose when in any competition, there must be a winner and a loser. You may hit back if you can.

Additionally, why is it that we keep flooding our shops/local markets with banana chips from elsewhere when we have bananas and can make our own banana chips? Why do we keep importing cheap products from elsewhere when we have material and labor to manufacture inexpensive products? My question is: Why are we still so stupid to be complaining about something we say is so good and necessary, something that if it continues will always result in one winning and the other losing? Why not rejoice with that country and ungrudgingly issue it with rewards?

Why not stop the complaints and simply come together in unity then organize and produce to take care of our people? We can and should always produce surplus to exchange for other products produced elsewhere in the rest of the world. We are all different, always will be and that is great. Why do we then continue to hate greatness?

There is no such thing as fair competition as no two countries or people are alike. Products that are said to be the same and grown or made in different parts of the world are not the same. The Jamaica Blue Mountain Coffee is the only product of its kind anywhere in the world as the conditions under which it is grown are unique or very different from the conditions under which coffee is grown elsewhere. It is therefore foolish to have coffee grown in Jamaica competing with coffee grown in Mexico. In fact, it is just as stupid to have coffee grown in St. Elizabeth Jamaica competing with coffee grown in the Jamaica Blue Mountains.

Pharmaceutical companies will not take too kindly to anyone advancing the use of natural herbs to heal diseases that they have been managing for decades. They will not allow the sale of their pharmaceuticals to dip. Through competition, information is sometimes withheld or amalgamated to ensure that such products continue to sell.

If a medical or law school has 100 spaces for students and 500 persons apply only 100 from that 500 who fiercely compete will win a space. Do you know some of the things some will do to gain admission? Some will pull on every possible string within their reach of influence to gain admission. It may be reaching out to politicians or any person in the institution who will do their bidding to gain the edge over another student who might be more qualified but has no contacts in the institution.

Anyone today who has a struggling business but can contrive a way in which to get help to keep the business running, will do so not caring about the source of the financial support. It is oftentimes called self-preservation, another name for competition. The very person who encourages fierce competition is also the very one who will ridicule you when you defy the odds or compete to save the business. Is this not the height of hypocrisy?

On the one hand they will say that if you do not vigorously pursue your own self-interest you will not make it. In fact, I will go further to ask: How will you then be able to win a spot on the television program Profile so it can be said, you see, it can be done and so many are doing it? Just be persistent and persevere, be persuasive, believe in yourself. If you can conceive it, you can achieve it.

When you can get all your tuition paid with change to spare as you were more cunning and competitive than another student, you win and the other loses. Why therefore is the loser ridiculed when according to the world's model, winning and losing are built into the entire economic/business model?

If your ganja plant is considered a threat to the economic viability of those planted elsewhere you will be prevented from growing ganja for as long as it takes to ensure that when your restriction is lifted, you will no longer be a threat to ganja grown elsewhere.

Your goats and cows will be taken by another farmer who currently owns goats and cows. Although it is called pradial larceny it is competition in disguise.

Is it craziness when one complains about the negative effects of competition yet in the same breath encourages competition as the only way to go to survive in this competitive world? For the writer it boils down to a world model that is plain dumb and stupid.

On September 23, 2014, I listened to a former Jamaica Festival Queen, Krystal Tomlinson's fat cow/meager cow competition analogy regarding beauty competitions in Jamaica as she engaged with the hosts of the Fresh Start 93FM radio program in discussing the choice of winners over the years in the Miss Jamaica World Contest. It was noted that many Jamaicans are usually vocal in registering their annoyance at the selected winner whom they would describe as being adorned with the features of a European. This chosen beauty would eventually represent Jamaica at the Miss World contest. It is thought that the choice is usually based on the judges' racial and physical concepts of beauty.

It was further aired that an African queen with darker skin and kinky hair should be selected as the more likely representation of Jamaica's African heritage. Immediately I formed an opinion that a meager cow competition would create just as much divisiveness as a fat cow competition. The wide array of darker skin and kinky hair is sure to create splits in the decision on a winner as much as the wide array in the European appearances. They are all so strikingly different and rightly so.

The winner is often influenced by the looks of the Miss World contestants who are mostly of "European descent". Hence, all others that do not have fair skin, long hair, thin lips, and straight nose must be eliminated to increase the chance of winning at the international level. I suppose one could say that the competition would be a much fairer one. However, I am yet to see a fair competition.

Krystal Tomlinson is a Jamaican female who won Jamaica's annual Festival Queen Competition in 2013. Her competitors were eliminated and had to be for her to have been declared winner. Elimination of any human on any grounds always creates divisiveness in relationships. No two persons are alike, have never been and never will be.

The world's population of approximately 7.5 billion people all have 7.5 billion different fingerprints. This is variety in all its glory and splendor.

Why is it that the winners of the Miss Jamaica World competition are mostly women with light skin, straight nose, and long hair? Everyone is special as the lyrics of a popular song indicate: "God made you special, God made you special, for there is no other who is just like you, special you are."

What good is competition among people who are unique? What good is competing when the result is the elimination of diversity? What good is competition except to create divisiveness, scarcities, violence, and crime? In fact, every conceivable evil has roots in competition.

In the sporting arena, the dynamics of competition is most divisive as it is indeed dynamic. Competition on and off the track's spreads far and wide incorporating sponsors, chemists, lab technicians, coaches, sportswear manufacturers, spectators and the list go on and on.

One athlete's unique ability in a discipline is enhanced by rigorous training, creating a star in that discipline. Rigorous training in the same discipline also enhances another athlete's unique gift. However, the second athlete can only attain first place to the delight of the spectators by way of the following:

False start by the favorite or fastest one in a sprint race resulting in their elimination,
The fastest one gets injured accidentally
Disqualification of the winner who used a performance enhancing substance

The latter also translates to competition among chemists to create a substance to boost performance without detection through random drug testing for substance abuse, by the sporting authorities. This is done to produce the win or arguably the upset win. There are times when the very rare occurs when two athletes share the win. The motivation behind such activities is always money and fame.

Competition imposes limits in the development of new discoveries as it eliminates many in the competitive field to award one or just a few winners. The drive brought to the table by losing contenders becomes clouded the moment they are eliminated. The loser would have lost out on a chance to discover purpose and progress to great heights by receiving a very small prize money or in many cases being eliminated without any reward. So, without the money to further develop the idea, it is lost. Under a collaborative work-based system which outlaws' competition, the incentives for new discoveries are propelled by our innate desire for better and the only incentive for better is better for all. We want to be comfortable, so we aim to find ways to achieve more comfort. As those ideas are brought to bear, they are acknowledged, explored, fleshed out and developed for common good. The better we seek; the better we will find which is already there waiting to be found or discovered.

Many potential good discoveries are untapped because under a monetary based system of competition, only those with the most money can seek, explore, and find, and having found it, it will then be sold at high prices which only those with money can afford. So, again many will lose out.

In Ecclesiastes 1:4, 9-11, Solomon says there is nothing new under the sun. What we are to do collectively is follow the Creator's advice, looking to the ants, the bees, the birds, the sea creatures, the plants and learn from their simple but masterful way of life for our own survival and sustenance. Search the scriptures in Job 12:7-10, Proverbs 6:6 and Jeremiah 8:7 for additional admonition to observe the tiny creatures to gain wisdom and understanding. We have done well at copying, but few have benefited because of the ugliness called money and competition, sadly seen by many as necessary evils.

Therefore, first case in point is that we should continue to look to our natural environment as well as good examples from experiences of our predecessors for solutions and use them to the benefit of all our lives.

George Bernard Shaw (Irish socialist dramatic and critic) stated, "There is only one sort of genuine socialism, the democratic sort, by which I mean the organization of society for the benefit of the whole people."

Franklin D. Roosevelt further expanded the sentiments when he declared that there is nothing mysterious about the foundations of a healthy and strong democracy. The basic things expected by our people of their political and economic systems are simple. They are:

- Equality of opportunity for youth and others,

- Jobs for those who can work,
- Security for those who need it,
- The ending of the special privileges for the few,
- The preservation of civil liberties for all,
- The enjoyment of the fruits of scientific progress in a wider and constantly rising standard of living

In 2015, Sharon Hay Webster a radio talk show host on Fresh Start program, News Talk 93FM reiterated that the Jamaica Blue Mountain Coffee is the best coffee in the world, and she went on to justify her statement by saying that our soil type is superior. I laughed out loud as such comment further solidifies the point that no two products created by two different sets of people or grown in different countries are ever alike. Our coffee is certainly different from every other coffee grown and produced in every other part of the world that grows and produces coffee. Additionally, no product produced by different sets of people are alike even if they taste alike.

So why compete? I answer, to eliminate diversity and to manipulate and control resources for the benefit of the few.

My friends and I went into a most popular food chain in St. Catherine and spent one thousand and eighty-five dollars on fried chicken, fries, etc. I felt for soup, but because soup was not sold by this food chain, I went next door to purchase the soup for one hundred and eighty dollars then rejoined my friends in the fried chicken shop. It is again very important to note that soup was not a part of their menu. Seated comfortably and about to raise the first spoonful of soup to my mouth, two security guards approached and indicated to me that the soup from the competing food chain was not allowed inside and so I should consume it elsewhere. So, here again was another moment of absurdities as I was being asked not to have a soup appetizer bought next door before consuming the fried chicken. Although both are food, they are totally different types and therein lies stupidity because variety is always the spice of life.

At a sporting venue, a discus thrower and a sprinter don't compete. Likewise, the sport of volleyball and football don't compete, yet they are all played at the same venue at the same time. So, I can only conclude they simply hated the thought of a different food product being consumed within their food shop, and how ludicrous. Chewing gum or candy is not on their product menu, yet I can chew a gum or eat a candy inside said shop. Why not also ask patrons with gums and candies not to eat such products inside as well? Are they not also purchased from competing food chains?

Nonetheless, my reaction was that I was very hungry and wanted to dine with my daughter and friend. I told the guards that the soup for one hundred and eighty dollars and the two boxes of chicken totaling over a thousand dollars were going to overrule the door sign, which I was not even aware of. I further opined that such a policy was most unfriendly, selfish, and very divisive.

I long concluded that most policies are never in the interest of customers. I knew I was right. I was proved right. I desired to sit and eat with my daughter and friend and having started I told the guards that I will remain seated to enjoy the whole meal especially as I wanted some of the fried chicken.

A supervisor was summoned to the table and I expressed the same sentiments while enjoying the food in the company of my daughter and friend. I immediately concluded that a similar sentiment would be communicated if we were to move to the other food shop. I was not prepared to sit outside to eat. I was also too hungry to move so I completed the meal and was however very careful to secure the soup container in its own separate bag as I had decided not to dispose of the Styrofoam in their garbage bin. I indeed felt a tingle of sadness for the security guards who behaved hurt and probably also felt nothing but shear hatred towards me as I did not adhere to their orders to either leave the premises or not partake of the soup. I can also hear readers saying that I was quite daring, and I am lucky to be alive to be able to write this narrative. Competition is indeed, evil as in this instance, it created contempt, hatred, hostility, and sadness over one medium soup and two boxes of fried chicken.

My friend on the other hand had to contend with coleslaw that contained hair particles sold by the said fried chicken shop. There were two visible strands of hair in the unfinished meal. We took the coleslaw to the supervisor, showed her the particles of hair, and indicated that maybe we need to get to the bottom of why we were served a meal that contained hair particles. I urged that the evidence needed to be secured at once because it will be most critical and important to ensure that the hair particles did not belong to either of us. Her response was simply that she would give us another coleslaw in exchange for the one containing hair particles. For a simple life, we took the replacement and left. Thank God we did not meet our demise by eating soup in a chicken shop to ease a natural hunger for food to live.

Competition is evidently about creating policies to separate, divide and rule and to create an atmosphere of hostility as competition is most unfriendly and knows not compromise in most instances.

Competition destroys variety and uniqueness. "Have some of my coffees for its uniqueness and I will have some of yours also for its uniqueness." However, when one competes against another, one is bound to take advantage of the perceived weakness of the other thereby eroding the spirit of cooperation and goodwill towards men.

Competition therefore is to try to kill off my coffee especially when it's so called third world so that only yours from a so called first world is available, and when demand is greater than supply then only your first world coffee will be available on the market where you can sell it for big money so you alone profit.

Competition is therefore about creating scarcities for the benefit of the few proving how stupid competition is in an also stupid capitalistic world. In this stupid capitalistic world, the creation of scarcities brings about huge profit and wealth to some stupid miserable egotists. The results are as exist currently; a world of complaints about some of the problems, complaints about the results from the problems and further complaints about the prescribed solutions, but no concern about fixing or eliminating the source of the problem. Therefore, everybody continues to complain.

COMPETITION AND GROWING OURSELVES OUT OF DEBT

Growing ourselves out of our debt is a worn out saying very popular in Jamaica today and elsewhere too. It is often said that we must compete with others to grow. Our indebtedness today far exceeds income that we have ever earned and will ever be able to earn. This is so because all people do not have the freedom to become educated to work to earn to grow ourselves out of our indebtedness as they compete. In addition, in our economic system people need to have money to educate themselves, to seek out or create employment to earn to grow. Moreover, it is a daily advertisement that resources are scarce.

Additionally, our loan repayments include interest which was never earned by anyone and can never be earned. In fact, interest payable is money that does not exist at all. Money loaned as principal, is the said money from which interest must be repaid, hence the need for competition. Therefore, as we all use principal to operate our businesses and compete for the scarce dollar, it is the said principal earned from competing that is used to repay loans. Others will need to enter the loan playfield to keep the loan ball active because more money is always needed to replace that which is won and used up by the few who always keeps winning due to their economic and political advantage. Losers will need to compete for the new loans coming into the pool to keep servicing their loans. There is never enough in the pool for all to win hence some must default on their loans. Also, the borrowing cycle is not always liquid hence those moments when loans are hard to come by many will also default on their loans especially those loans with high interest rates. Many will also need to consolidate, and others will simply go bankrupt. So, having to borrow money then compete with other borrowers to service high or low interest rate loans does not guarantee success. Also borrowing money to pay for one's education does not guarantee success or the freedom to succeed and grow oneself out of debt.

This means that freedom and money are diametrically opposed. Louis D. Brandeis, a US Supreme Court Judge stated, "Democracy is not possible in a monetary based economy therefore one cannot play by the rules to succeed in a monetary based economy." Brandeis also said, "We can either have democracy in a country, or we can have great wealth concentrated in the hands of a few, but we can't have both." Wealth concentration is usually in the hands of the smaller percentage of every population who fears no rule.

To grow as a people means we must work as a people. However, if those in authority continue to tell people that we cannot work without money, be it to acquire the tools or implements to work or be it the lack of money to pay the people after work, then we will NEVER grow. If one cannot acquire education without money, then we will also not grow.

Governments in Jamaica and the world over, change hands, election after election. In each administration the following issues are constantly advanced, "We lack the resources to pay salary increases to all classes of workers, teachers, doctors, the police et al. We lack the money to repair our roads, bridges, hospitals, and schools. We lack resources to convert inner cities to winner cities, run pipes for potable water to all people and to provide electricity to all people. There is lack of money for all people to live. This is very critical as many people die from illnesses due to the lack of money to pay for total health care or the attention from a medical professional and or hospitalization. Without health there can be no wealth, hence money is the silent weapon of mass destruction.

Jesus Christ while on Earth many decades ago always restored people to good health, freeing them to go forward to work Working is a necessary good for all. Money on the other is an evil designed to confuse, control, and create work exemptions for some. Confusion and control lead to unnecessary misery, stress and ultimately death.

The National Water Commission on the other hand controls water, which is life. In fact, the Commission boasts that water is life. It is the Creator who blesses us with life, water, and food to sustain life and not the National Water Commission. We must work to multiply and replenish the supply of potable water and food. The National Water Commission says not so, your life is dependent on money which you need to earn somewhere and pay us to get water in your pipes. Also, if you are lucky to work for us, after we pay you, you need to pay us back the money for the water that your work produces. Sounds confusing? Yes, it is confusion. We need to work for money and then use that money to buy our life despite the fact we already work to produce said products that we are buying back. The hoax and destruction are that without you being paid that money, you will not get water hence you will steal, kill, become ill then ultimately die a slow and miserable death much to the delight of those who profit from your demise. If you don't die, grave diggers, coffin makers and funeral homes will not earn money. How grotesque and undignified to earn money from death and destruction.

Take a careful look at those Earthlings who continue to spread such lies that one needs money to live or survive. They all have water, food, best homes, and modes of transportation to their comfort all the time. Those who endorse such lies and still have no water etc. are dangerous fools.

To love money is to love life. If money is tied to life, then there is no stopping the things people will do to continue their lives. Would you kill for money if your life depends on it? Can one's life really be dependent on money?

One needs to make an urgent decision on the part one will allow competition and money to play in one's life. Will you conquer money, or will the love of money conquer you as you compete and eliminate your competitors?

PART 4: SCARCITY AND ELIMINATING IT

It was interesting to hear the late Ian Boyne agreeing with his Neuro Linguistic Programming guest on the television interview program Profile on Sunday December 28, 2014, when he indicated that, the very subject and practice of economics is based on scarcities.

We are reminded of scarcities every day, and it seems to be never ending. Every country has an economy of creating goods and services and an intricately designed mechanism for making them available to satisfy the demands of consumers. Very prominent on the list of scarcities frequently discussed in the public domain are jobs, skills, food, water, equipment/machinery, houses, medicine, teachers of mathematics, agricultural support staff to assist farmers and very laughable 'money'.

Another concern is not having enough doctors in some specialty areas to serve in clinics and hospitals across the island. Sometime ago it was bemoaned that only three cardiovascular surgeons were in Jamaica to serve several hundred patients with cardiovascular diseases. The concerns were that patients requiring the related surgical care were growing constantly among a population of approximately 3 million people.

Funny it is that everything that is scarce first requires the input of people. Yet well recorded is the fact that unemployment and idleness among people in Jamaica and the rest of the world is astronomically high.

If machinery is needed to perform jobs, only people can design and manufacture the machinery. The resources, which the earth provides can be mined, replenished, and used by people to produce the equipment. Therefore, the people must somehow be engaged to produce. Nothing happens by chance. How therefore can the machinery or equipment needed to produce food or medicine be scarce when people, land and material from the earth are available to the very people?

How can houses be scarce, when there are people, land, and material available in the earth and above the earth to build houses? How can doctors or nurses be scarce, when there are people available to become doctors or nurses? How can RADA officers be scarce, when thousands of people who need work can be trained to work and earn? How can teachers of mathematics or any other subject be without jobs, when illiteracy abounds in Jamaica and the rest of the world?

How can money be scarce, when any quantity of money can easily be conceived in the mind of man and the very man himself can decide how much of that money he will print as currency on pieces of paper for circulation into the system? Paper is produced from processing trees or species of grass namely bamboo. Bamboo is not just available in abundance in the earth but has a faster growth rate than any other tree or species of grass. Note too that the materials to manufacture the very printing machines are also available in abundance in the Earth. What is the catch in complaining about the very things for which the answers or solutions lie an arm's length away?

I received the information below on December 25, 2014 and every year at the same time since then on my smart phone, reminding those of us who have the following things to realize how much better off than most of the rest of the world we are. Note too that the rest of the world includes people in every part of the world, not one country, nationality, kindred, or tongue is excluded; be it Singapore, Sweden, Finland, Canada, China, and other countries described as doing extraordinary. It goes as follows.

"If you have food in the refrigerator, clothes on your back, a roof over your head and a place to sleep you are richer than 75% of this world. If you have money in the bank, in your wallet and spare change in a dish some place you are among the top 8% of the world's wealthy. If you woke up this morning with more heath than illness, you are more blessed than the millions who will not survive this week If you never experienced the dangers of battle, the loneliness of imprisonment, the agony of torture or the pains of starvation you are ahead of 500 million people in the world. If you can attend a church meeting without fear of harassment, arrest, torture or death you are more blessed than three billion people in the world. If your parents are still alive and still married, you are very rare even in the United States of America. If you hold up your head with a smile on your face and are truly thankful, you are blessed because the majority can, but most do not. If you can hold someone's hand, hug them, or even touch them on the shoulder, you are blessed because you can offer a healing touch. If you can read this, you are blessed more than over two billion people in the world who cannot read at all. Count your blessings. Is this the type of world that is at times branded as doing well with statistics of scarcities like this to be taken seriously as really getting better? Very contradictory indeed and I wonder who wrote it and if that person has material wealth.

Nigeria has been branded a very wealthy country, rich in resources especially oil. So, Nigeria seems not to have a lot of scare resources if it is branded wealthy. Agreed? I am very sure the Nigerian people are considered one of the richest resources that Nigeria possesses. Do you also agree? The people of every country are the richest resources of such countries, wouldn't you say?

However, it has been observed and noted by Dr. Phillip Wilcox, retired ambassador for counter terrorism in an interview with Mrs. Sharon Hay- Webster and Errol Lee on the Jamaican Radio Talk Show Fresh Start on January 11, 2015, that the leadership of Nigeria was not ensuring that all the Nigerian people benefit from the rich resources that the county possesses. This can be said of Jamaica as well as many other countries.

On the one hand, there is abundance of wealth but on the other hand, the Nigerian people lack wealth. People are considered the richest resources in every country and people are extraordinarily resourceful. So, one is left to wonder, how then can there be scarcity of jobs, professionals and money in Nigeria or any country for that matter.

How do the leaders of every country spread the country's wealth to the benefit of its entire population? How does the leadership of every country ensure that the resourcefulness of each citizen benefits the other which would allow for common good?

It is obvious that someone is therefore lying or misleading the people or both and it begs the question; who is lying or misleading the people and why?

I must also share this piece of information heard on the very same Fresh Start program on the morning of December 29, 2014 where a telephone guest said to the two female hosts: "Ninety-five percent of land in the world is owned by white people and men". Is it an easy task to calculate the very small percentages of whites and men who own almost all the land on the Earth? The Earth was indeed created for man, male and female. How did man and whites come to own nearly all the Earth?

There exists lots of discrimination in the world the main ones being, people described as whites, thinking themselves superior to those described as blacks and men thinking themselves superior to women, and then all the other discriminations sit under these two main umbrellas. People with lighter shades of skin feel superior to people with darker skin shades and are treated as such. Those who live uptown think themselves better than those residing downtown. Some think others look ugly and not fitting for certain jobs while those with professional degrees think themselves better and brighter than those without similar qualifications. The very long list of discriminations which are far too many to mention include those in government who think that they are god overall and the rich thinking themselves better than the poor.

However, back in the days of slavery the discrimination was mainly black versus those described as whites. The slaves, regardless of their nationality or skin color (lighter skin, darker skin) all worked for the whites. They survived all the hard labor without being paid a dollar for many years. How did they survive without being paid? Well, they had the air from which they got oxygen freely. They had food to eat as they were constantly required to farm agricultural produce and they had water to drink as they tended the wells. They had somewhere to live as they were also construction laborers who built houses and lived in them along with their masters.

The very basic but most critical needs which are food, water, air, shelter, and clothing were all met. This tells me that one does not need to be paid to survive. We instead need air which is free and abundantly available to all. We need food which will be available for us to eat if we cultivate it. We need shelter from the harsh elements, and we need water without which we will all die.

Water is also available freely. It also tells me that we do not need to be paid to do any form of work. The slaves back then with different skin shades all worked and survived without being paid any form of money. The one inequality is that their slave master did not work. The slaves ate the very food they farmed and so did their slave masters. The slaves helped to build the houses they occupied as well as those lived in by the slave masters. The slaves operated the water wells, and all drank water as did their slave masters. The slaves-built roads and travelled on them and so did their slave masters. This does not mean that the same slaves that operated the water wells also built the roads, or the same set of slaves farmed, etc. However, everyone including those who did not work benefited from the collective labor of all slaves who worked very hard.

This reminds me of the unexplored precedent set by the Israelite Joseph in the Bible story on collective labor. Joseph was commissioned to lead Egypt by the Pharaoh at a critical time of seven years of pending food shortages. However, before the famine, there were seven years of plenty. Joseph must have engaged the skill set of every citizen including himself in Egypt to work for the benefit of all. This led to supplies of food for all of Egypt plus a vast surplus of food kept in storehouses built to precision at right temperatures etc. to feed the rest of the world. Can this be repeated in islands rich in natural resources such as Jamaica?

The Earth with all its resources including the environment, when properly managed will provide life's necessities for all. It did back then during slavery. It did back then for the Egyptians under the leadership of Joseph as well. Ecclesiastes 5:9 says, "Moreover the profit of the Earth is for all; the king himself is served by the field."

I am not in support of slavery in any way, shape, or form. I do not support some people working to support others who refuse to or are not allowed to work I am in support of working to eat bread and all should work because all must eat to survive. Therefore, there is everything right about working.

We are all to work as was ordained from the very beginning. Man was told by our Creator to be fruitful and multiply and replenish the Earth and subdue it; and have dominion over the fish of the sea and over the fowl of the air, and over every living thing that moveth upon the Earth. Read it in Genesis 1:28 and Genesis 2:15. This scripture shows variety as the spice of life. Having dominion over the fish of the sea could be the marine biologist, the fisherman, the regular sailor, or captain of a ship. Other occupations include the farmer, the chemist, botanist, the architect, the plumber, the garbage collector be it man or woman, the doctor and the list go on and on to include every single occupation found on Earth today.

Every individual on Earth has a contribution to make and all should be allowed to make such contributions to eliminate scarcities. It should be a matter of policy for all to work. With people being busy there would be very little idle time for mayhem and mischief.

Back in the Bible days after the Pharaoh was afflicted by the seventh plague, he granted permission to Moses the leader of the Israelites to take them into the wilderness to offer sacrifices of worship to Almighty God. Several days after the pharaoh became struck by the fact that although they had in essence, money and other forms of wealth in abundance, the actual work that was required to allow them to keep and increase this wealth so they could continue to enjoy the high life of sheer partying and drunkenness could NOT be carried out by all the wealth they had. Money and wealth do NOT work. Money and wealth cannot produce more money and wealth. People work to produce. In fact, 'let your money work for you', is a lie. It is let people work for you while you sit lazy and be paid money. Only people work with hands and heart, so Pharaoh needed the Israelite slaves.

Pharaoh had only two options: to make new slaves from among his own people or to go after the Israelites to continue their enslavement. He chose the latter. So, Pharaoh immediately marshaled his army to pursue the Israelite slaves to take them back by force to sweat and labor so they could continue their lavish lifestyle. The Bible tells of the parting of the Red Sea which eliminated Pharaoh and his army. Could this be repeated in Jamaica?

The slave masters and the Pharaoh still exist and are just giving orders and living healthy, wealthy lives. Who are these slave masters? Today, if we do not have money, we cannot eat, drink, communicate, travel, live in houses, and so on. However, I am far more concerned about the very three necessities for life which are air, food, and water.

It is often said by many that if all the air could be captured by man, it would be done so it could be sold for money to other humans. The very utterance suggests that I am not the only one troubled by the fact that sometime back in the distant past, men were able to successfully carve out a way to keep the bonds of slavery, discrimination, manipulation, and control intact. This allowed them to do as they pleased with the Earth's rich resources, causing frustration and misery to other humans.

The Scriptures say in Ecclesiastes chapter eight that one-man ruleth over another to his own hurt. Although the air is used by men to spread diseases and unleash weapons of mass destruction on people accused of being a threat to security, it still cannot be mined by the few to fully control and manipulate the many. However, food and water have been manipulated and controlled using money, leaving dark corners for those without this resource. The very lives of human beings have been tied successfully to money. From this we get scarcities, discriminations, and slavery. Note too that it is almost impossible for a mind that is not properly nourished by the consumption of the various food groups, to be at its creative best. The result will be malnourished bodies and minds.

Physical slavery was abolished but was immediately replaced with economic slavery using money as the controlling force. We now need to emancipate ourselves from economic and mental slavery to eliminate scarcities. Having this important knowledge, how do we do such?

We start by instantly seeing ourselves the way we are different from each other but undeniably connected to each other. How are we connected to each other? If you believe that we were all made in the image of God, then we are all connected originating from the same life source. However, if you believe we evolved from a nonliving organism according to Darwin's evolution theory, we are also still connected originating from one source. Whether you choose to believe Darwin or God, we are all connected. Therefore, because we are connected, the approach to eliminating lack must be a connected or unified approach.

Moses recorded in Genesis that God populated the Earth with an abundance of varied life-giving resources, sustained by incredible cyclical phenomena in the sea, on land and in the atmosphere. Psalm 104:5 tells us that God laid the foundations of the Earth, that it should not be removed forever. "Behold God is great, and we know him not, neither can the number of his years be searched out. For he maketh small the drops of water: they pour down rain according to the vapor thereof: which the clouds do drop and distil upon man abundantly." Job speaks to the vein in the earth for silver, gold and brass molten out of stone. We are told in Job 28:5 that our very bread cometh out of the earth and under it is turned up as it were fire.

Nothing was in scarce supply at the beginning of creation to sustain life. The Earth today contains the same life sustaining resources and cycles that work in order, harmony and precision albeit compromised because of sinfulness. We have abundant sunshine, which ensures plants and vegetation flourish to provide food for every living thing human or non-- human. "As for the earth, out of it cometh bread" (Job 28:5). We have water, the most abundant substance on Earth; we have the air we breathe. The seasons come and go without any alteration. "He appointed the moon for seasons: the sun knoweth his going down" (Psalm 104:19). There is therefore no need for scarcities or competitions. "Who lay the foundations of the Earth, that it should not be removed forever. He sendeth the springs into the valleys, which run among the hills. They give drink to every beast of the field: the wild asses quench their thirst. By them shall the fowls of the heaven have their habitation, which sing among the branches. He watereth the hills from his chambers: The Earth is satisfied with the fruits of thy works. He causeth the grass to grow for the cattle, and the herb for the service of man: that he may bring forth fruit out of the earth; and wine that maketh glad the heart of man, and oil to make his face to shine, and bread which strengtheneth man's heart. The trees of the Lord are full of sap; the cedars of Lebanon, which he hath planted. Man, goeth forth unto his work and do his labor until the evening" (Psalm 104:23).

What we need to do, is to work collaboratively to take care of, manage and preserve all the resources in our shared space for continued sustenance. How do we work? "But ask now the beasts, and they shall teach thee, and the fowls of the air, and they shall teach thee: Or speak to the earth, and it shall teach thee: and the fishes of the sea shall declare unto thee" (Job 12:7-8).

So, although we are all connected, we were created different as God would have it. God is not boring in the least; hence he created varieties in every species. Any from the human species that discriminates against another based on differences in skin shades, hair textures, etc. are stricken with the worst form of mental illness that is anti-God and anti-humanity. Such a people easily are deficient in wisdom, knowledge and understanding or simply possess an inferior IQ. It's confusion about life and living. it's confusion about the true meaning of different shades, colors and varieties which are important to the normal development of one's spiritual sense of discernment. It's a disgrace to humanity and all life forms and such people should never be looked on as being racist, but rather as abnormal and clearly needing an injection of wisdom, knowledge and understanding to release them from the dumb state that they have been in for centuries. God has given all different and exciting gifts to contribute and manage Earth's resources for common good. Hence, we need each other to work collaboratively to satisfy every unique need of humankind and eliminate lack without eliminating variety.

To further substantiate the above points, the Bible in 1 Corinthians 12:14 states; "For the body is not one member, but many." Likewise, we are many people but one Earth to live in, to be sustained by and to sustain. Hence, all have a contribution to make and should be allowed to contribute. Verses 15-26 state; "If the foot shall say, because I am not the hand, I am not of the body: is it therefore not of the body? And if the ear shall say, because I am not the eye, I am not of the body; is it therefore not of the body? If the whole body were an eye, where was the hearing? If the whole were hearing, where was the smelling? But now hath God set the members every one of them in the body, as it hath pleased him. And if they were all one member, where were the body? But now are they many members, yet one body. And the eye cannot say unto the hand, I have no need of thee: nor again the head to the feet, I have no need of you. Nay, much more those members of the body, which seem to be more feeble, are necessary: and those members of the body, which we think to be less honorable, upon these we bestow more abundant honor: and our uncomely parts have more abundant comeliness. For our comely parts have no needs: but God hath tempered the body together, having given more abundant honor to that part which lacked: that there should be no schism in the body; but that the members should have the same care one for another. And whether one member suffers, all the members suffer with it; or one member is honored, all the members rejoice with it". This is variety in all its glory. What an awesome Creator.

The elected Government or leaders in our country and every country are therefore all connected having no more rights to Earth's resources over anyone else. They are from the people and elected by the people to serve and complement the other members of the body and therefore they are not separate and apart from the people but are instead a part of the entire body of people.

We are therefore all dependent on each other for the health and well- being of the entire body. Governments should not render hardships in taxations and the famous lack of resources towards its other members creating pain, fear, and insecurity while they are enjoying the best of Earth's resources. Such is evil and not to be tolerated by citizens because there are more than enough resources for all to benefit from. "Depart from evil and do good; seek peace and pursue it" (Psalm 34:14).

What sense does it make for the fingers to say to the nose, I value more than you or the foot to the brain I value more than you or the ears to the eyes I can do without you, but you cannot do without me? It's totally absurd when all are of the one and same body.

The white man is of no more importance than the black man or the Indian man or the Chinese, and neither the doctor more important than the garbage collector. We are all human beings and all human beings whether black or pink, whether doctor of garbage collector, Indian or Chinese need the same air, water, and food to survive. Bob Marley and Marcus Garvey both echoed; Until all people recognize that none is superior by the hue of the skin there will be war. And with wars come divisiveness, scarcities, a fall and ultimately death. We either unite and stand or divide and fall.

THE EARTH

The Earth belongs to all. Ecclesiastes 5:9 states, "Moreover the profit of the Earth is for all: the king himself is served by the field". Every piece of commodity that is produced, be it machinery, furniture, equipment, food, or accessories comes from the earth and all people of the Earth must be allowed to produce by the sweat and labor of all, according to their gifts and talents. We are all totally dependent on the Earth for our life, livelihood, and sustenance. It is only logical and reasonable to require that all Earthlings participate in work as a beneficiary of Earth's resources. All who can work should work.

"The Earth also is the Lord's and the fullness thereof, the world and they that dwell therein" (Psalm 24:1). God who owns the Earth and places mankind in it requires of us to take care of the Earth as it takes care of us.

We are told to be fruitful and multiply and replenish the Earth, to take care of the plants and animals on the Earth. We are told to keep and to dress the Earth.

Therefore, we have been hardwired with the necessary skill set and abilities to manage Earth's resources for common good and as such should do accordingly. The only way to create abundance, equality and to enhance our relationship with each other is for all to work for each other and for the sustenance of the Earth. It is said in 11 Corinthians 8:14 that, "But by an equality, that now at this time your abundance may be a supply for their want, that their abundance may also be a supply for your want: that there may be equality."

A great lady Ellen G. White in her book, Councils on Education, gave very good councils on good stewardship among the sexes and the spin-off effects to the society at large. Mrs. White lauded the life of the greatest man ever to walk this Earth as follows: "As Jesus worked in childhood and youth, mind and body were developed. By his own example he taught that it is the duty of every man, woman, and child to be industrious, that our work should be performed with exactness and thoroughness, and that such labor is honorable."

Jesus was a carpenter. He had a skill and he worked at his skill. The exercise that teaches the hands to be useful and trains the young to bear their share of life's burdens gives physical strength and develops every faculty. "And the child grew, and waxed strong in spirit, filled with wisdom: and the grace of God was upon him" (Luke 2:40).

All and not some should do something that will be both beneficial to themselves and to others. God appointed work as a blessing and only the diligent worker finds the true glory and joy of life. The approval of God rests with loving assurance upon children and youth, boys and girls that take their part in the duties of the household sharing the burdens of fathers and mothers. Such children will go out from the home to be useful members of society.

As such, the long-held practice of competing one against the other where one wins and the other loses must be eliminated. The monetary system must be scrapped as it has served the purpose of destroying good and is of no benefit or relevance to anyone but more of a hindrance for collective good. Moreover, the monetary run economy breaches the constitutional rights of citizens. How so? Our Jamaican (Constitution) Order in Council 1962, Chapter III, Fundamental Rights and Freedoms 962 guarantees us the right to life as follows:

Whereas every person in Jamaica is entitled to the fundamental rights and freedoms of the individual, that is to say, has the right, whatever his race, place of origin, political opinions, color, creed or sex, but subject to respect for the rights and freedoms of others and for the public interest, to each and all of the following, namely: life, liberty, security of the person, the enjoyment of property and the protection of the law; freedom of conscience, of expression and of peaceful assembly and association; and respect for his private and family life, the subsequent provisions of this Chapter shall have effect for the purpose of affording protection to the aforesaid rights and freedoms, subject to such limitations of that protection as are contained in those provisions being limitations designed to ensure that the enjoyment of the said rights and freedoms by any individual does not prejudice the rights and freedoms of others or the public interest.

No person shall intentionally be deprived of his life save in execution of the sentence of a court in respect of a criminal offence of which he has been convicted.

Without prejudice to any liability for a contravention of any other law with respect to the use of force in such cases as are hereinafter mentioned, a person shall not be regarded as having been deprived of his life in contravention of this section if he dies as the result of the use of force to such extent as is reasonably justifiable in the circumstances of the case - for the defense of any person from violence or for the defense of property; in order to effect a lawful arrest or to prevent the escape of a person lawfully detained; for the purpose of suppressing a riot, insurrection or mutiny; or in order lawfully to prevent the commission by that person of a criminal offence, or if he dies as the result of a lawful act of war."

However, the monetary system and its monetization of everything on Earth replace our fundamental right to life with its requirement for us to have money to use as a means of survival. In essence, with no regard for our constitutional rights and freedoms, the creators and suppliers of this money have set themselves above us and have thrust money upon us as the only means by which we can benefit from Earth's abundant resources of food, water and clean air on which our very lives and their lives also depend. Who are these people? Where did they come from?

It is quite reasonable to assume that our right to life guarantees us equal rights to the resources on planet Earth. We can only benefit from Earth's abundant resources when work is applied to mine said resources.

It therefore means that there must be organization of collective labor among all of Earth's people to mine said resources and convert same to satisfy all needs. It also means that the creators and suppliers of this money must be rejected. They must also become a part of the collective labor like everyone else to mine Earth's rich resources for all our survival.

So, under the current monetary based economic system, it is fair to assume that the more dignified way to acquire money would be through work, and because there is no law that guarantees work for all citizens, then our rights to life is highly compromised. Imagine too that under our existing economic system, it is mandatory for all citizens 18 years and older to register with a scheme called the National Insurance Scheme (NIS) to guarantee them a pension at the age of 65 and beyond. However, one will not receive pension benefit unless they contribute money to the scheme. Again, the most dignified way to consistently acquire money to contribute to this mandatory scheme is by being employed. Being employed is not mandatory or guaranteed. This is yet again clear proof of the evils of a monetary based economic system which clearly is a hoax and a system of sabotage and therefore must be rejected.

Democracy or the freedom of the people to be and to do cannot be dependent on money. Democracy is not possible in a monetary based economy. Money therefore needs to go so there is no hindrance to human progress.

Currently, money is used primarily as a tool to take freedom away from people; freedom to even protect oneself against unhygienic assaults. People are not allowed access to the basic life-sustaining necessities especially potable water due to the lack of money. Taking away people's freedoms is to uproot purpose and stifle prosperity. To stifle prosperity is to create scarcities.

Money is also used to create inequalities. It is used to limit people's movements. Without money, you might very well not be able to attend school. It is used to compromise the education system. Without it you may very well not be able to sit important examinations. It is used to create and reward laziness among all peoples, nations, kindred, and tongues. Consistent hand out of money to people without jobs may very well eliminate their desire to engage labor to earn an income. The lack of money has exposed families to discriminations, separating parents from their children as property owners refuse to tolerate children in their rented properties. The lack has resulted in one and in some cases both parents migrating to a foreign country for more rewarding employment opportunities destroying the family unit, destroying morality.

During slavery, the slaves labored and sweated in the earth and were not paid. However, their slave masters were paid money for not laboring. Today, a great majority earn millions without working while those who labor away in the fields are paid next to nothing.

An athlete, a cricketer, or any sports professional can earn billions of dollars playing sport for entertainment while factory workers who produce the winning athletic gears faint away in factories from poor nutrition due to underpay and adverse working conditions. There are those who are robbed and murdered by others who do not work.

Money does not, cannot and will not build athletic gears, build roads, plant food, give water or electricity to Earthlings. Money does not give life and can never take life. People kill and murder. Inactivity and laziness inspire people to take life to get money for their life. Economic prosperity for all can never be achieved with money when money that is required for the very prosperity, is never available in the amounts required. This is sheer hoax.

It is absurd to hear citizens agreeing with those who have created this satanic system that places monetary values on plants, people, and animals. A cow can be of more value than a goat simply because the demand for goats may be more than the demand for cows. Or a pig is worth more than a rabbit because more people prefer pigs. All animals are totally different in appearance, purpose, and behavior. Whether one chooses cows, pigs or rabbits does not diminish their importance or their unique use and value to us and there need not be an assigned monetary value. God the Creator gave us humans, male and female, the authority to rule and manage the Earth and its contents. Therefore, if one hundred citizens want goats and only fifty are available, then breed fifty more goats. If seven persons need rabbits and only one is available, organize and make six more available. On the other hand, there is no need to overproduce pigs if pigs are not needed. If there is a need or demand for mandarin derived from a tangerine, then engage in further agricultural exploits as God granted us dominion so we should simply collaborate and satisfy the demand for mandarin making it available in the quantities that are required to satisfy the need.

Everyone, yes everyone needs to work to fill all the diverse needs that exist for every product. As diverse as the people are, so diverse are the needs of the people and all such diverse needs can and must be met when all participate in work. Work must always be complemented by rest. With our levels of intelligence, we can plan in anticipation of the needs for every product and produce accordingly. And if we did not do very well and are caught off guard, we learn from such experiences and make the necessary adjustments and improvements. Remember, we are human beings and will err from time to time.

We are in charge and can therefore increase or decrease production when necessary. It is done all the time but only to benefit a few. We can also create varieties because the Creator has given us authority. We must therefore be faithful stewards and create abundance to fulfill our needs by collaboration and not by competition. When we collaborate, we produce more for everyone. The principle 'do unto others as you would have them do unto you is best served through collaboration and not competition. "But by an equality, that now at this time your abundance may be a supply for their want, that their abundance may also be a supply for your want: that there may be equality" (11 Corinthians 8:14).

The existing laziness and many wanting to reap what they have not sown is because of a monetary run economy. Many have not sowed a seed in their entire life yet reap bountifully in the name of working smart. Again, the very slave masters could be so accused as they did not work. The slaves did all the work, and their masters became wealthy. The slave masters then used the very same money to re-employ the very slaves paying them very little, even withholding some of the wages already earned.

In fact, under the current system, the unnatural synthetic paper currency we call money is used to re-value the very natural resources found in the earth from which the money or paper currency is made. The money is also used to value human, and machinery built by said human to create currency. This is absurd. Money is elevated over both human and machinery in that the survival of human and the manufacture of machinery has become dependent on said money. The patent holders have also long discovered how to create money without the use of labor and machinery and conferred upon themselves exclusive power and authority to do so. However, paper currency is continuously printed and still requires labor and machinery. The production of machinery can be labor intensive. Many lives have been lost from mining activities that occur at great depth below earth's surface to replenish material required for maintaining machinery and equipment. It is also absurd that those who labor under such strenuous and dangerous conditions, whether to facilitate the creation of currency or contribute to a clean livable environment which enhances the quality of life for all, are not paid enough currency to significantly benefit from their intense physical labor. For example, intense labor assists the development of the material used to fill a cavity in a tooth. A worker will neglect his own dental health due to his very demanding work schedule and most likely will not earn enough to be able to pay the dentist to maintain his own oral health. So, he now suffers from an unattractive smile and bad breath which expose him to embarrassment because some moron says he must have money to pay a dentist who they claim is an even more valuable human being by virtue of his field of study.

Morons are stupid men who invented and created monetary currencies from the resources on Earth using same as a tool to manipulate and control both man and labor, creating a disconnect on Earth which has led to crises, discriminations, abuses, and scarcities. Poverty is one of the most disastrous consequences from the actions of morons.

God, the supreme owner of Earth and all it contains, during his sojourn on Earth showed us the key requirements to restoring better relations among Earth's population by being a God for the poor and needy. God came to a world steeped in inequality and misery. However, God was a God for the sick, the blind, the paralyzed, the deaf and those with poor oral hygiene. God was extremely big on health and wellness. He would heal the sick restoring excellent health without a coin being paid for such service. He then gave the command, "Go and do thou likewise." Obviously, the removal of discriminations is a clear start to discovering one's purpose.

Simply, to eliminate scarcity we must all be rid of discriminations and be allowed to discover and develop our diverse purpose in service to each other. Solomon declared, "Go to the ant thou sluggard; consider her ways and be wise. Which having no guide, overseer, or ruler, provideth her meat in the summer, and gathereth her food in the harvest. How long will thou sleep, o sluggard? When wilt thou arise out of thy sleep? Yet a little sleep, a little slumber, a little folding of the hands to sleep: So, shall thy poverty come as one that travelleth, and thy want as an armed man." We must understand that we can no longer listen to talks of scarce resources because the aim of the talkers is to keep poverty intact. We cannot remain divided when we are all connected to each other as one people created in the image of one God and herein lies the basis of human equality.

Get this! Every commodity that money is used to acquire is produced by people and as people produce, people will consume. Therefore, as people develop and find their true purposes in life every necessary skill, trade, job, work, or profession, will be filled by people to ensure abundance in all the various products needed for survival.

To assist, the discovery and development of skills would require access to all existing learning environments and institutions currently available to mankind. Everyone should be allowed exposure to all subject areas and a variety of skills, based on their natural love and ability to grasp one or more. The purpose of this freedom to learn and express is to achieve one's purpose for oneness, as the Godhead is one in purpose. Some might have a short tenure while others will remain for longer periods. However, at the end of tenure, everyone would have an acquired skill or skills.

If people can do what they are good at doing and love to do, this can only mean good not just for that individual but good for the collective. Some people will grasp and function in multiple subject areas and skills while others will learn and grasp less. This is the reality of this life. Our eyes only see, and our ears hear while our feet walk, run, jump, kick and even write. Eyes, ears, and feet are all important with their diverse skills and functions.

All would have access to the basic needs of man, which are clean air, clean water, nourishing food, clothing, and shelter. Those who have an affinity for the science of tree grafting to produce varieties, water purification, pipe laying, farming, architecture and construction and other skills would naturally gravitate and develop. Contractors need to be taught and their teachers need houses to live in. Those who engage in the production of houses need food to eat and those who produce food need houses to live in. Those who get sick need the doctor and the doctor needs equipment to diagnose the illness. The engineer who designs the equipment and machinery needs the doctor, a house to live in, food and water just like everyone else. Those who are so skilled will produce accordingly while having their needs met by others who are producing what they need. All would therefore be at work in their own field and loving it as they serve each other. Simply we all need each other, whatever our gifts, skills, and contributions. As everyone is allowed free access to every known current skill set and profession on the Earth, they will find their calling, and will perform at their optimum with joy and gladness in their hearts. Each one teaches one becomes manifest. It is stated in 11 Corinthians 8:14 that, "But by an equality, that now at this time your abundance may be a supply for their want, that their abundance may also be a supply for your want: that there may be equality".

"We are a people of courage who can proclaim; let us do something very different today; right now. Let us simply be free as free, and not using our liberty for a cloke of maliciousness, but as the servants of God" (1 Peter 2:16).

We must also recognize that we cannot make our lives better without God as our supreme leader and Creator of everything including the Earth and the land without which we cannot create products for our very levity. "O Lord, I know that the way of man is not in himself; it is not in man that walketh to direct his steps" (Jeremiah 10:23).

So, we identify lands in all fourteen parishes as determined to be suitable for residential purposes as well as all forms of productive activities such as agriculture, mining, manufacturing, and commerce.

All persons should also be given land in all the fourteen parishes according to their current family size and needs. All are entitled to their privacy to do as it pleases them in their own space, not infringing and being a menace to their neighbors.

We should conduct meetings throughout the island to elect two leaders each and 14 deputies for all fourteen parishes to collaborate and plan with the people. There should be a gender split of eight women and eight men, a total of 16 for each parish. Genesis 1:26-28 says, "And God said let us make man in our image after our likeness and let THEM have dominion over the fish of the sea, and over the fowl of the air, and over the cattle, and over all the Earth, and over every creeping thing that creepeth upon the Earth. So, God created man in his own image, in the image of God created he him; male and female created he them. And God blessed them, and God said unto them, be fruitful, and multiply, and replenish the Earth, and subdue it; and have dominion over the fish of the sea, and over the fowl of the air, and over every living thing that moveth upon the Earth."

Our court system would remain, having judges and lawyers, because wayward people will from time to time require interventions and judges to preside over issues and render judgments. However, judges and attorneys are not exempt from getting involved in other pursuits. It will never be perfection because if sin remains on Earth there will be challenges of all sorts, but life can certainly be better than it currently is.

Joseph's leadership of Egypt as chief minister during a time of scarcities, created enough resources for the Israelites and Egyptian people with surplus that also fed the rest of the world. The creation of abundance in Egypt is also used as precedence for administering our current affairs of creating abundance through work by all who can work starting right here in Jamaica land of paradise. We will sell all surpluses to the rest of world for money if it is prudent to do so. We in turn, can then buy, or make exchanges for anything we need and are not able to produce.

Joseph created abundance and eliminated scarcities. We can and must do the same. At the time the Pharaoh appointed Joseph Prime Minister of Egypt, he declared that not one of his people will suffer or be in want. Not one Jamaican needs to be without food, shelter, or clothing.

Firstly, it must be established and agreed on by all, that producing enough food or goods and services to satisfy the needs of all people, is good. Secondly, for abundance in supplies to be achieved all or most of the people must be in one accord, embracing the thought that good is good for all. God is good and is only found in good. The devil is evil. Evil is derived from and found in the devil. For those who prefer evil and the devil we could give them their own devil's paradise.

Joseph was able to use God and good, which means abundance to eliminate the devil and evil which means scarcities. Those who prefers evil may also create evil in abundance for themselves by themselves.

Every single person in Egypt who could work, no doubt worked to create abundance to last the seven (7) years of famine. Joseph must have engaged the skill sets of all the workers in Egypt so that services would be rendered by all and for all. Just imagine engineers designing new farming implements, laborers using implements to clear the lands and planters sowing seeds. Imagine irrigation specialists at work to ensure that the seeds are watered, laborers at pains to eliminate choking weeds and others removing them for disposal. Those who like to reap where they did not sow would then be reaping what was sown by others. However, what is reaped would not be for their benefit only but for the collective.

Imagine designers designing storehouses for the reaped crops and chemists and mathematicians at work to ensure that temperatures will be right to prevent grains from going bad in the storehouses. Contractors are setting up to start construction. Drivers are carefully using heavy duty equipment. Cutters are cutting stones; miners are mining sand and marl. Others are reaping herbs or plants and butchering animals for consumption as cooks are preparing food for everyone to eat and stay healthy. Doctors are always on call to assist those who fall ill. Here is your chance to continue the process to eliminating scarcities.

CROSSINGS

Crossings are a way of life sometimes smooth; Sometimes they cut like a knife
We must grow and change to survive, for Crossings brings a new way of Life.

Taste changes as the days go by
Baroque style came but crossed over in the twinkling of an eye Neo-Classical to the mid-19th century saw simplicity, grandeur, and lots of symmetry.

The Earth quakes and shakes constantly Buildings changes and are built differently.
It's a crossroads with many directions Cross over, keep moving is it not your intention?

Churches are no longer Gothic You are human, so don't stay static
Cross over the bridges and experience the thrilling sensations new ideas, new likes, new passions
The dictates from generation to generation.

PART 5: DOES GOD LOVE YOU?

Can you name one person or thing that you love? I bet you can. How about the God in whose image you were made? Do you love him? He loves you. "For God so loved the world that he gave his only begotten son, that whosoever believeth in him should not perish, but have ever lasting life" (John 3:16).

In love God created you and he created you also to love him in return. "We love him because he first loved us" (1 John 4:19). However, your desire to love and serve God is all your choice as God created you with the freedom to choose as such is the nature of God. His nature is not a dictator over humans but rather giving humans freedom to choose. However, he desires you choose wisely because he knows the consequences of all choices whether good or bad. You have the choice to love others as you love yourself.

How easy or how hard is it to love others? Did you know that your love for that person or thing, despite the differences, reflects God in you? "Beloved let us love one another; for love is of God; and everyone that loveth is born of God, and knoweth God. Love is not by chance. He that loveth not knoweth not God; for God is Love" (1 John 4:7). So, if you love which I'm sure you do, surely you are God's indeed whether you chose to believe or not.

Imagine, you have a choice to believe or not to. But tell me; is there a negative in believing and accepting truth? In this was manifested the love of God towards us because that God sent his only begotten son into the world, that we might live through him. Herein is love, not that we loved God, but that he loved us and sent his son to be the propitiation for our sins. Beloved, if God so loved us, we ought also to love one another. This sounds good to me, does it sound good to you?

No man hath seen God at any time. If we love one another God dwelleth in us, and his love is perfected in us. Hereby know we that we dwell in him, and he in us, because he has given us of his spirit. And we have seen and do testify that the Father sent the Son to be the savior of the world. Whosoever shall confess that Jesus is the Son of God, God dwelleth in him, and he in God. And we have known and believed the love that God hath to us. God is love, and he that dwelleth in love dwelleth in God, and God in him.

Herein is our love made perfect, that we may have boldness in the Day of Judgment: because as he is, so are we in this world" (1 John 4:17).

If you are still reading, this certainly is another demonstration of God's love for you. You are reading because you have the gift of sight. The gift of sight is so amazing and should at no time be taken for granted. Is that not love? There are some who no longer have sight or were born without sight. However, they do have other gifts such as hearing, touching, feeling, and tasting. Those who have lost one or more of such gifts may ask the question: If God loves me then why has he allowed me to be blind or deaf? This is a very good question to ask. First, I must tell you this. Did you know that God's plans for you is to live forever, to never get sick or die? Did you also know that God changes not and therefore such plans remain forever? Yes, I know so many have gotten sick, and many have died. And so, you further question, did God not love them? Of course, God loves all.

Earlier we mentioned that we have choices in all this. Yes, you can choose God and live or you can choose Satan and die. No, it does not mean that all those who have died chose Satan. They are dead because the wages of our choice to sin even once is death, but the gift of God is eternal life to all those who choose to believe and accept that gift from God. Therefore, although you may die, you will live again.

Adam and Eve did not die the moment they sinned, well at least not physically. Adam lived after he sinned nine hundred and thirty (930) years. Therefore, death does not mean instant physical death. I am happy I brought in the point of Adam and Eve as it leads me here. When that first Earthly pair disobeyed God they yielded to the temptation of Satan and so chose to give up God's rulership over their lives and their home in Eden. In that moment, Satan became their instant ruler on Earth. Had they continued to choose God as their ruler, to listen and obey him, they would have kept their home in Eden. They would have filled the Earth with children no doubt including us today and there would be no sickness or death. With choices come consequences. Just imagine!

So, sin entered and right up to now Satan is still the prince of the Earth occupied by us today. 11 Corinthians 4:4 reads, "In whom the god of this world hath blinded the minds of them which believe not, lest the light of the glorious gospel of Christ, who is the image of God, should shine unto them." Can you now begin to understand why our friends our families and ourselves get sick and die? Because Satan brings separation or independence from God the only life giver, and once there is separation from God there is death. God is life, God is love.

The moment Adam and Eve obeyed Satan over God; there was instant separation from the life giver. Everything under the dominion of Adam and Eve also became affected and all that came after them including Cain, Abel, and every son and daughter born after, right up to this very moment including all of creation; animals, birds, insects, etc., were also affected. Today, every disease, sickness, motor vehicle accident, murder, and such the like are created and set upon us by Satan's dominion of Earth and our hand in choosing his leadership over the leadership of God. So, sickness and death intervened and make it appear that God's original plan for eternal life for humans will never again happen. Wow, surprise for you, God's love for you and I is still at work even with our denying God by choosing Satan and death. This is amazing, what love? Here is why. John 3:16 a scripture in the Bible you may very well be familiar with tells us what God has done to demonstrate his love for us. It reads, "For God so loved the world that he gave his only begotten Son, that whosoever believeth on him should not perish but have everlasting life". When we sin, we are condemned to die as referenced in Romans 6:23 and Genesis 2:17.

However, God decided that he was not going to leave us to die the eternal death, but he was going to take the punishment for us instead. This is a tremendous gift for us to ponder and show our eternal gratitude for. Imagine committing a crime and standing before the judge in court who pronounced the sentence of life in prison or of death by lethal injection. Then by some turn of events your sentence is changed to freedom from imprisonment or death? God overturned your death sentence to life everlasting and so it is yours for the claiming. God loves you and it is his desire for you to live and live and live, be happy and healthy forever.

However, life everlasting cannot and will not be in this Earth in its current form. I repeat, you cannot experience everlasting life, the absence of sickness, death, hurricanes, accidents, disappointments, etc. on Earth in its current form.

God's plan for us cannot be accomplished under the rulership of Satan. While Satan is ruling Earth, how can you expect to have a life of total ease? Under Satan's rulership, there is sickness, diseases, accidents, disasters, a monetary system that creates shortages of jobs and money to buy food, medicine, and an endless list of essential items. All this, including the destruction of Satan must end before you can be the beneficiary of eternal life. Yet amazingly many are blaming God for all the disasters mankind now faces in a world dominated by evil.

We must choose whether to continue to blame Satan or God. Satan knows that his time is now short. He is at work in a mad hurry. It is his delight when you cast blame on God for all his evil creations that you choose to partake in.

But listen up my friend, God is certainly not going to help Satan to continue lying to you that his rulership of Earth is superior to God's rulership. If you make the choice to smoke and drink which will clearly damage your health and God clearly warns you against abusing your body, then you will reap what you sowed; an unhealthy and sick body which will eventually die. Also, being exposed to secondhand smoke will affect your health as the bad decision of one does affect others under Satan's rulership. If God was just to snap his fingers and your health returns then would it not be that God is endorsing Satan's way of rulership; that anything goes, you can use and abuse your body without any negative consequences? My friend that is just not possible.

You are also aware that one bad move, intentional or unintentional can have an impact on many persons. One person can light a single match and burn down the homes of an entire community. Imagine you take a gun and blow your neighbor's brains, and then the relatives of such neighbor decide to do the same to your family members. Did you expect that God would relieve you of your freedom to choose and stop you from doing evil, making you into a robot after he has clearly given you the freedom to choose not to engage with a gun? God changes not and you cannot have it both ways.

There has been a proliferation of systems in running Earth; communism, socialism, democratic socialism, capitalism, and others. Governments come and go as the choices are made, one man over another man or a woman, all promising better but giving us more of the same and worse. Joblessness continues, crime and violence continue, monetary issues worsen, and people continue to die from sicknesses and diseases of all sorts.

Amidst all this turmoil the love of God is still available to you. Evil and the devil are also present. However, good and God are available and abound even more. Clearly there are only two choices, good and evil. How and what will you choose, God and his goodness or the devil and evil?

Choose God and you get love, for love is of God, and God is love. God loves you.

Did God create the man to rule the woman and the world? God did not create a weaker sex, man did.

The teaching which continues inside and outside the church is that God created the man to rule the woman, the world, and all that is in the world. Genesis 1: 26-28 speaks with the cleanest clarity of God's intention and purpose for man. Man means both the male and female whom God created on the sixth creation day.

God gave male and female, side by side, authority to rule the entire world together. In Genesis 1: 26-27, God said, "Let them have dominion over every living thing that moveth upon the Earth. And God blessed them, and God said unto them, be fruitful, and multiply, and replenish the Earth, and subdue it: and have dominion over the fish of the sea, and over the fowl of the air, and over every living thing that moveth upon the Earth." Plainly, God did not create the male to rule the female and the Earth.

God is omniscient; he knows all things. He knows the end from the beginning. "Before Abraham was, I am" (John 8:58). God knew before he created the angels that the angel Lucifer would sin and create evil. God knew that Lucifer would be the first deceiver. God knew Lucifer would use the serpent as an instrument of evil to deceive Eve. God knew that Eve would be deceived. God knew that Adam would follow Eve blindly and eat the forbidden fruit.

Adam was not the one to have been mysteriously led away or be deceived by Satan who used the serpent as a mask and a cover. 1Timothy 2:14 speaks: "And Adam was not deceived but the woman or female being deceived was first in the transgression."

God knew that Adam would then blame Eve the woman for his choice to follow her and sin against God. Adam like Eve was hardwired with the same abilities to reason and to utilize the special gift of freewill God gave them both. Adam could have chosen to use his freewill differently; to honor God in that most critical time.

Adam did not. He also refused to take responsibility for his own decision and action.

God knew the impact that Adam's blame on Eve would cause for generations to come. God also knew that human relationships were going to be badly affected because of the fall by Adam and Eve. In fact, God told Eve what was going to happen. God told Eve that her desire was going to be to her husband, and he was going to rule over her. Here, God DID NOT tell Adam to rule over Eve. In Genesis 3:16, God simply told Eve what the outcome or the consequence of her action would be. Man would constantly blame woman for sin and not its inventor Satan. He would also present himself as having authority to rule over woman while struggling to exercise control over his own selfish desires. God also revealed his plan of salvation for Adam and Eve and the entire human race in Genesis 3:15.

God knew that men would have followed in the footsteps of the father of deception. God knew that men would similarly deceive and distort the written word just like Lucifer did in distorting God's word. "But in vain they worship me, teaching for doctrines the commandments of men" (Matthew 15:9).

Matthew 15:14 states, "Let them alone: they be blind leaders of the blind, and if the blind lead the blind, both, shall fall into the ditch." Matthew 7:15 also notes, "Beware of false prophets, which come to you in sheep's clothing, but inwardly they are ravening wolves."

Man has imposed his own authority over the world and has both attempted to force and have forced some women into submission. God did not create robotic human beings at any time. After sin, both male and female remain free, moral beings; free to accept and worship God only or not to. "For God so loved the world that he gave his only begotten son that whosoever believeth in him should not perish but have everlasting life" (John 3:16). However, man has constantly claimed that the woman is his robot and she must do as she is told, especially within a marriage. Some have said that, had Eve listened to Adam her husband, it would have guaranteed her not being exposed to Satan and becoming deceived. In other words, her worship and honor were to be towards Adam's while Adam's worship was to be God's. Since the head of the man is Christ and the head of the woman is the man, it would similarly follow that man was also created as God's robot, and had he listened to Christ, he too would not have sinned. Therefore, he should not have exercised any freewill and followed his wife into transgressing. How did he being God's robot not follow God's instructions? Lucifer tried to impose his own authority on all the other angels in heaven to usurp God's rights to rule heaven and Earth and was cast out from heaven along with one-third of other sons of God who sided with him according to Revelation 12:7-9 and Luke 10:18. Clearly, all the angels were likewise not created robots but with freewill to choose who to love and obey or not to love and obey. This obviously points to a God who desires obedience and worship from a freedom of choice and not by forced submission.

Man, again imposed his authority and rules over his own gender with much anger and hatred. The statistics today of men murdering their brothers play out the last part of Ecclesiastes 8:9 with astounding accuracy.

Satan hated Jesus and successfully influenced the hearts of men to kill him according to Luke 23:1-56. In Matthew 17:22-23, "The Son of man shall be betrayed into the hands of men; and they shall kill him and the third day he shall be raised again." Today whatever the murder figure is, the majority are male murdering another male. They murder women and children too. They execute women and children out of their desperation for revenge and some are possessed with distorted sexual cravings where at such times they rape and then murder. Are they more concerned to subject women to do their bidding rather than subjecting themselves to do God's righteous bidding?

Eve's desires were for Adam to do good to her and her to him, but the modern-day Adam rules over women and abuse almost one out of every four females on Earth. Throughout Bible history it is very clearly recorded that men ruled over women and treated them like commodities.

The sin of polygamy in which men took unto themselves many wives, was introduced by a man named Lamech. In Genesis 4:19, Lamech with senselessness like that of Lucifer decided that he wanted more than one woman and took two for wife. This is a characteristic of Satan in that he is never satisfied with anything, the more he has the more he wants. Today many men express openly their desire to have more than one wife as a possible solution to the current economic crisis. One woman is a complete woman just as one man is a complete man.

Men senselessly set about to plunder women and girls right up to our times today. They prostitute women and girls in exchange for man-made money. One sinner ruling over another sinner is never a good thing, says Solomon in Ecclesiastes 8:9. God therefore clearly did not create man to rule woman before or after sin.

Women's desire of men today is for men to do good, to reason the things out according to God's will and desires. In other words, God desires man to right the wrong done by the first man Lucifer using God as his guide. God desires us all to love him and love our fellowmen as we love ourselves as endorsed by the apostle in Matthew 22:37-40.

Sin has its beginnings in man. Ezekiel 28:15, Genesis 4:8 and Romans 5:12 speak to this with clarity. Pain, hardship, thorns, and thistles were all because of the fall of Adam and Eve. Weakness was also a result of man's sin. God did not create a weaker sex. Genesis 1:31 and Solomon in Ecclesiastes tells us that God created everything good and upright. Mankind sinned and created weakness and a weaker sex. So, when the woman is referred to as the weaker sex, such has its genesis in sin and disobedience. Men continue to subject themselves to the will of Satan the father of all lies. Satan hates a good relationship and so he has been quite successful in messing up human relationships by using the blame game. Men also continue to blame women for so many wrongs that the very man casting blame is guilty of.

Today, many daughters and sons blame mothers for the absence of the fathers in many homes. If the father continues to claim headship and rulership, why is he missing in action?

Men have certainly distorted the leadership and headship they conferred on themselves and have submitted to selfishness, love of power, fleshly desires, and pride. Men have the biggest egos. They ill-treat and look down on women and some even resort to thinking and calling women the inferior gender. Some on the other hand are blaming women for thinking themselves inferior to men.

Today parents are encouraged on the one hand to love and treat equally all their children; sons and daughters alike. Yet so many men do not recognize or treat the woman as their equal.

Sin distorts, corrupts, separates, steals, is utterly selfish and only seeks power and self-gratification, as in patriarchy and the boys' clubs.

Man and woman working together as one with God as the supreme leader and ruler will defeat sin and prosper.

"Two are better than one; because they have a good reward for their labor" (Ecclesiastes 4:9).

Solomon was certainly not talking about two males Adam and Steve but surely male and female in partnership working together as one in Christ Jesus.

"There is neither Jew nor Greek, there is neither bond nor free, there is neither male nor female: for ye are all one in Christ Jesus" (Galatians 3:28). Likewise, in a marriage, there is no more male of female but one body as the two become one in purpose.

IS IT A MAN'S WORLD AND WHY? WHAT'S WRONG WITH THE WORLD?

The information presented below to support an affirmative answer to the questions asked, may not be palatable at the onset. However, I have no doubt that as the information is closely examined bearing in mind the huge impact males have had on shaping the world, many will finally agree that not only is it a man's world but that what's wrong with the world is man.

Very arguably as well, is that in substituting what is wrong with what's right with the world, I have to say that the answer would be quite like what's wrong with the world. Easily, man or male is also what's right with the world.

Being able to fix 65% of the wrongs in the world, could easily lead to a significant fix on a fair share of most of world's problems.

Men have always sought to rule and dominate the world and the implications of this can be seen in a world past, present and future. A world filled with wars, strife, confusion, hatred, greed, competition, anger, and despair, and lacking in very basic reasoning for the good of all, has been a great force to reckon with.

Just consider the following: Satan has been presented in the Bible as the prince of this world. John 12:31 states, "Now is the judgment of this world: now shall the prince of this world be cast out." Paul in 11 Corinthians 4:4 writes; "In whom the god of this world hath blinded the minds of them which believe not, lest the light of the glorious gospel of Christ, who is the image of God, should shine unto them." John in Revelation 12:7-9, 13 and Revelation 13:18 continues, "Let him that hath understanding count the number of the beast: for it is the number of a MAN; and his number is six hundred threescore and six."

Most countries are under the rule or leadership of men. Hence men create almost all our laws. This has led to the never-ending creation of more laws with each creating new problems and very little solutions.

The current monetary based economic system was conceptualized, implemented, manipulated, and is managed by males. It is one of the Earth's greatest ills among all nations, peoples, and tongues. Many of the Earth's people have been fully brainwashed mostly by men, to believe that it takes money to fix roads, to build houses, to create jobs and to do just about everything. The word resources are used from time to time as a substitute for the word money. The people are told and reminded every day that resources are scarce, hence very little can be done for roads, housing, water, etc. This phenomenon has been around for centuries. It is the same today and so it will be in the future, especially against a background of mounting monetary indebtedness. The Bible states that God's people are destroyed for lack of knowledge. Man says we need money to acquire knowledge, become educated and to survive. However, said money is placed far out of reach, that even our most basic needs for clean air, water, food, and shelter are hindered. Learning becomes difficult on empty stomachs.

Men also created the male dominated sporting arena and the players are called professionals. It is a very high-paying profession, perhaps one of the highest paying professions, and it creates a slew of rotten rich individuals who use their wealth to acquire sheer vanities. Just imagine being paid billions for playing around on a field wasting sweat and muscles romping rough. And for the sport of boxing, such is the creation of serious bodily injuries to the delight of spectators and ultimately slow death from sustained injuries. This is shear insanity. Sporting recreation is good but not of the type that dominated in the past and currently obtains.

As with many professions that exist in the world, men in most cases are paid more than women, even when the women do as good or an even better job than the men. In fact, men work less and are paid more.

It is my belief that men of influence more than women refuse to acknowledge the existence of the God of creation, the Creator of all things good and the superior intelligence behind the Earth and the entire universe. I am also inclined to believe that men more than women, refuse to be accountable to anyone especially to God.

All armies in the world are dominated by men. Most murders are committed by men; men killing other men, women, and children. Examine the murder statistics in Jamaica and the world and you will see. Rapes, child abuse, abductions, child marriages and incest are perpetuated and executed mainly by men. Men practice child marriages in many countries. Do you know of one country where women marry little boys?

In a few countries and several cultures, men can have as many wives as it pleases them and can afford financially. Men believe money will get them anything they desire. They believe they own everything and that anyone they spend money on is their property.

A man will father as many children with as many women as it pleases him and goes about his business with very little or no pressure from other men to support his offspring.

The gun, a weapon of mass destruction used daily to wound, cripple, and kill other men, women, and children, was first developed by a man and is used more by men to do harm. It is said that 95% of the world's prison population is comprised of men.

The first sin, the first murder, the first deception, in fact all evil had its beginnings with HE. Read about it in the Bible, a book that has the most printed copies in almost every country, nation, and tongue.

The entire history of the Bible features and mentions more men than women in every aspect of life. Men are far more influential than women especially in doing evil. Conversely, men could be even more influential in doing good.

As I listen to the lyrical content of a song entitled "I Would like you and my Sweetheart to be Friends," I am reminded of how very insulting men are to women and the effects of such insults on women. History has proven that women accept their insults in the similar way that a puppy dog that is mistreated remains militant for more insults. The song by Beenie Man, "Man fi have nuff gyal, nuff gyal in a Bundle" is so rooted.

There can be no doubt that men are quite influential when it comes to evil and wrongdoing, which is very abundant and as the saying goes, "One fool makes many." It started with Lucifer in heaven and one-third of the spirit beings defected and were eventually cast out of heaven.

Look at gangs, the smoking of weed and taking hard drugs. It takes very little doing on the part of a 'don man' to gain the following of a line of boys. Men love to gang rape and commit murder in revenge for the simplest of reasons such as not repaying a debt or returning a minor loan as low as J$50 or a gun.

It is said and so far, proven in a court of law that Dancehall DJ artist Vybz Kartel fits this bill of committing murder because it is alleged that a gun belonging to him was not returned. I would dare say that most men in Jamaica think that Kartel is a lyrical genius and are behind him in support of some of the senseless lyrics he chants. In fact, one such senseless lyric appeared to have assisted his murder conviction.

I make no apologies for what I write as I am prepared to say all that I have to say without even an ounce of fear. I have no fear of any senseless man not even the very devil himself. I fear only the true and living God. All who kill or murder will indeed join the dead eventually.

Men do influence women in very negative ways. They have negative influences over women and children to the extent that after the committal of a vicious act of rape or carnal abuse by a man, the abuser's mother, grandmother or close friend will excuse the behavior as; the man just having a little sex. In fact, both men and women often say; men cannot help themselves sexually.

Take a keen look in the churches today. Most churches are headed by men. Many are false prophets. Many commit acts of rape and other crimes and are still able to garner and receive support from both women and other men world over. Then, look at the lives of the women against the statistics of poverty, joblessness, rape, and physical abuse in the very churches. One out of every four women is abused by a man it is said. Consider the 2014 figures of reported cases of molestation in Jamaica. Go research and see for yourself.

An unrepentant Jezebel in the Bible masterminded murder in the worship and support of her husband's greed to own land. King Naboth desired land next to his and his offer to buy said land was denied by its owner. His wife Jezebel, in honor, reverence and worship of her man was livid that her god was denied fulfillment of his desires and took matters into her own hands. During the rule of King Ahasuerus, Haman the king's appointed prime minister was also worshiped and supported by his wife to commit murder to have her husband's desire for power and fame manifested.

Again, I will refer to Vybz Kartel on the issue of man's overwhelmingly negative influences on both genders. In watching an interview with Winford Williams on his TV show On Stage a few years ago, Gaza Kim Hamilton a guest on the show declared that she had no idea why four men beat her up at the Kartel Empire. The interview was done shortly after Kartel's conviction for the murder of his own friend Clive 'Lizard' Williams. She said that Kartel walked by her and saw her crying from the beating his men gave to her but ignored her. It was further said on the show that Kartel later publicly declared that he had no knowledge of the beating and he does not support abuse of women.

In watching the interview keenly and listening to Hamilton's unstable utterances I was more than convinced that she chooses to live in fear needing no freedom to be herself. She is pleased with her monetary achievements from her associations with Kartel. She was happy to use the On-Stage platform to tell the world and remind herself in an abundantly clear voice that she thinks very highly of Kartel and had forgiven Kartel for ignoring and denying her cry for comfort while she suffered pain caused by the beatings by his men. Forgiveness is always good and must be complete. She did not indicate however if she had also forgiven her abusers. She made no public declaration on that count.

Her life she owes to Kartel as she declared that if it were not for Kartel, she would not have had an opportunity for fame and fortune in the entertainment industry. It sounded and had all the markings of idolatry.

Popular dancehall artiste Black Rhino declared on On Stage as well, that he had no knowledge of Kartel's Love for guns or gun involvement as he referred to such as Kartel's personal life and he had no knowledge of Kartel's personal life. He however declared his reverence for Kartel and considered himself Kartel's very good friend. In fact, he indicated that they had been friends from high school days. He shared that Kartel is a genius. Kartel asked him for advice and to him that was something unheard of. Rhino questioned his own worthiness and capabilities to give advice to Kartel. He however indicated that he did break away from Kartel and his men. Nonetheless he too like Kim demonstrated low self-esteem in my opinion and has joined the ranks of idol worship found in manly fear.

"And it seems to me perfectly in the cards that there will be within the next generation or so a pharmacological method of making people love their servitude and producing...a kind of painless concentration camp for entire societies, so that people will in fact have their liberties taken away from them but will rather enjoy it, because they will be distracted from any desire to rebel by propaganda, brainwashing, or brainwashing enhanced by pharmacological methods." - Aldous Huxley, 1959

Now, can you just imagine how taking on the task of fixing men would change the entire world from a man's world to a world for all? This would be the biggest revolution ever witnessed by the entire universe. But can we hold our breath on this one?

So, men commit acts of murder in our society almost daily. They molest and abuse women and children daily and the loudest outcry of society today is we need very special prayers for our children. Is it that we need special prayers for our children for the purposes of them running away to escape the abuses of men or to escape parental abuse? Where or who will they run to? Or is it that we need special prayers for our men that God will grant them the minds to render good to our children and not drive them into prostitution and a life of neglect and crime? Is it that we need special prayers for our men that God will grant them minds rendering good to women and other men? Imagine that this would be the change that God has always wanted for men. Is this not one of the many reasons why God in the person of his son Jesus spent so much time with men in his sojourn here on Earth over 2000 years ago. Is this the man's world?

When will the world of men and women return to equality and oneness just as the Godhead is? "Let us make man in our image, after our likeness and let them have dominion over the Earth" (Genesis 1:26).

Should God have meant that he created a man's world as now obtains then I guess he would have made Adam and Steve? But did he?

PART 6: THE HE DOMINANCE

God created powerful spirit beings before he created human beings. These spirits beings were referred to as sons of God in Job 38:7. Psalm 8:5 calls them angels. Human beings have also been called the sons of God as 11 Corinthians 6:18 reads, "And will be a father unto you, and he shall be my sons and daughters, saith the Lord Almighty." Galatians 4:4-7 refers to humans as adopted sons of God.

Two differences between human beings and spirit beings are:

1. Spirit beings are invisible to human beings today but not the other way around. However, before sin, Adam, and Eve the first Earthly human beings communicated face to face with God. The Bible says God is a spirit and those who worship him must worship him in spirit and truth.
2. Spirit beings or angels do not procreate. Human beings have the gift of procreation.

However, a most profound similarity between spirit beings and human beings is: Both have freewill to do, whether to serve and worship God the life giver or to serve and worship self or other gods that mankind creates. Both spirit and human beings have hearts, voices, eyes, feet, and other bodily similarities. The human you can see, the spirit being you cannot see.

Most of us by now have heard of the famous spirit son of God named Lucifer. Lucifer was a he who exploited his freewill. We have also heard of Gabriel who used his freewill only in service to his Creator in Luke 1:19, 26-

28. Daniel talked about thousands and ten thousand times ten thousand of other spirit beings. Wow! That sounds like millions of spirit beings all with freewill.

It is my belief that a God who quite obviously loves variety as seen in his creation, would also have created spirit daughters of God as well, but then it begs the question: How comes we have not heard any mention of a spirit daughter throughout the account given in the Bible? This is a reasonable question to ask. I think an equally reasonable answer would be that the spirit sons of God covered both masculine and feminine just as man means male and female.

In the human realm God created man. However, man was gifted with procreation, hence; God distinguishes between male and female because male's role in procreating is different from that of the female. Angels do not procreate hence there being no reason to distinguish between spirit son or spirit daughter. It should not however be read as any foregone conclusion that angels are all he as is projected by many.

Very significantly, the angel who defected was named and identified as Lucifer a son of God, and further called by all the male pronouns - he, his and him. In Genesis 2:22-23, the female is referenced as her and she and the male he, his and him. Lucifer is also referenced he, his and him throughout the Bible.

My theory is that there is no specific mention of these spirit daughters of God or a calling out of a She because not one of these spirit daughters turned themselves into a devil. Further, I believe that none of the spirit daughters of God sided with the spirit son of God, Lucifer, who turned himself into the devil. The he or Lucifer ascended into the limelight by trying to usurp his Creator hence the obvious focus is on the he Lucifer who both created and became evil.

The angel Gabriel and many other good spirit beings that appeared to humans as recorded in the Holy Bible, have also been called out and described as he. In my humble opinion, this is consistency as the he became dominant and continued throughout up to current times. God had no desire for sin or evil. However, sin did not catch God off guard. God had a plan to defeat sin and restore good. God executed the plan as Jesus died and defeated sin and the devil that created sin. God has freely offered us the same victory over sin and the devil.

Angels appeared to Abraham, Lot, David, and Daniel. An angel appeared to Balak and Jacob who it was accounted wrestled with an angel. An angel also appeared to Mary at the empty tomb of Jesus and told her Christ was already arisen. All such angels were described as he. Lucifer was referred to as the man spirit being in Isaiah 14:16 which states, "They that see thee shall narrowly look upon thee, and consider thee, saying is this the man that made the Earth to tremble, that did shake the kingdoms?" God appeared and spoke to Abraham as an angel in Genesis 22:11-12, "And the angel of the Lord called unto him out of heaven and said Abraham and he said here I am. And he said, lay not thine hands upon the lad, neither do thou anything unto him: for now, I know that thou fearest God, seeing thou hast not withheld thy son, thine only son from me."

The Bible tells us that one-third of the angelic host in heaven sided with Lucifer's betrayal against God and God's authority to rule the universe. All one-third I believe were spirit sons of God and all he. "And there was war in heaven: Michael and his angels fought against the dragon; and the dragon fought and his angels and prevailed not; neither was their place found anymore in heaven" (Revelation 12:7-8).

Again, my theory is that if there were spirit sons, there were spirit daughters too. However, I think if a spirit daughter had challenged God's rulership or even sided with Lucifer a spirit son, it would have been quite significant in heaven and there is no doubt in my mind she would have been called out and the Bible would have been written very differently. Men are featured significantly in the Bible. Jesus, the son of the Godhead during his sojourn on Earth chose 12 disciples who were all males. The focus primarily remains in the 'he' realm instead of she because He assumed and outlawed God, He loved and assumed power and glory unto himself over God.

He Lucifer deceived Eve. He Lucifer created the ultimate separation of the Godhead. He Satan is the god of this world as stated in 11 Corinthians 4:4 and Luke 4:5-7. He Lucifer tore apart the Godhead. Jesus cried on the cross, "My God my God why has thou forsaken me?"

The world's first murderer was Cain. He killed his brother Abel. Joseph's own brothers having first contemplated murder sold him to strangers who sold him into slavery.

Then He in the triune God (Jesus Christ the son of God) stood up triumphantly to the he Lucifer (Satan) who sought to challenge the rulership and authority of the Godhead. He of sin was permanently defeated by the He of righteousness. This is a God who deals righteously.

A third of the angels in heaven cast down to Earth, have been working continuously to ensnare men and women. Statistics on criminal and violent activities prove that the males are more receptive to evil spirits to perform evil. Males commit by far more acts of violence than females. These violent acts are in no way limited to just one gender. However, men committing violence against other men far exceed men committing violence against women except for sexual abuse which is primarily committed by men. Similarly, men are their own worst enemy. For example, while men will complain about their women being unfaithful in relationships, they are the very same men desiring and engaging their own brethren's women and refusing to stand up in defense of their brothers in situations where women are the aggressors. Also, men will side and strongly support other men in perpetuating a patriarchal society. Men in leadership positions are totally responsible for the many failures of men in our societies today. Men are the heads of governments, churches, colleges, universities, and all the institutions that assume power to create laws, shape policies, educate to make real men and yet statistics show that more men abandon their responsibility in fathering their sons and daughters. More men are involved in gang warfare, in fact it is so bad that a male song writer penned a lyrical piece no doubt from desperation that "God just need a few good men". All such occurrences definitively justify the He dominance albeit with far too many negatives. If you have a more credible explanation, please do not hesitate to share.

I was also quite curious as to the reason Lucifer set eyes on Eve over Adam, to try to win her support to side with him in his accusations against God. It appears to me that because he had no luck in negatively influencing God's spirit daughters in heaven, he had to try elsewhere on Earth for a human being support. I am of the belief that that was the primary reason Lucifer selected "she" in the human pair as his target because he theorized that therein was the challenge. He slandered God using trickery, deception, and all manner of lies to Eve. She listened and became caught off guard with the fanciful and dazzling use of the serpent. Wow, this was the most beautiful talking serpent holding and eating the fruit that God told her would cause her death the day she ate it, but Eve saw that the serpent was very much alive as he ate the forbidden fruit. Sadly, she became overly captivated with the lies from the serpent, lies that had an appearance of truth. She made the choice to submit to the lies and her husband under no deception partook in the lie.

Today, men similarly deceive women. A very popular deception is when teenagers are conned by men into sexual grooming. In fact, men's desire to indulge their sexual appetites with children instituted the era of sexual consent at 14 years old and now 16 years old. Again, this clearly points to the male dominance. Why else would there be an age of sexual consent for children attending high school? It is such a man's world, that no power except the collective power of men could change the age of sexual consent to 18 years or older. The male is indeed dominant. Men's obsession and immature desire for power and submission is more in line with the brainwashing that women are to be under the rulership of men. Men are quite obsessed with being sexually pleasured by young children whenever they so desire to be pleasured.

It is very easy to reject any argument popularly advanced by men that Eve was the weaker sex and so it was easier for the devil to tempt her into submission. That line of argument of women being the weaker sex to submit to Satan is man's invention. The origin of weakness came from a sinful man and not a righteous, strong, and loving God. God the upright Creator did not create weakness or weaklings in his creation. Ecclesiastes 7:29 quoted a wise man as saying that all he has found out is that God created man (male and female) upright, but men have sought out many inventions. The ruling of man over woman is an invention of man. God told Eve about it in his direct address to her found in Genesis 3:16. God was speaking directly to Eve and not to Adam.

Another destructive invention by men in my opinion is the payment of taxes to man for the use of God's world. This reminds me of the widespread trade that took place in heaven when Satan who is the author of the monetary system and the system of taxing sought to assume awesome power over God's property in heaven. Lucifer viciously lobbied the angels who sided with him against God and bought votes amounting to one-third.

Eve fell to the persistent but quite foolish and senseless temptation from Satan. She then offered Adam the forbidden fruit and he too very sadly ate although not subjected to any form of deceit. He thought that blaming Eve for giving him the fruit would relieve him of his lack of self-control to resist partaking in sin.

Men today senselessly adopt one of the unfortunate legacies left by Adam. Men are always ready and willing to blame women for everything they lack the will to exercise control over. They will senselessly or without reason commit an act of evil. Adam was not deceived and therefore had no reason to commit the evil act in eating the fruit that Eve offered him. Adam exercised his God given freewill, ate then blamed Eve.

Rapists are famous in using excuses such as the ladies are to be blamed as their dress mode compelled them to take that which was not offered or given them. Men like the devil have a "teki" mentality to take what has not been offered them. I wonder what their excuse is for sexually molesting toddlers and kindergarteners who not only have no responsibility for how they dress but are unable to defend themselves. Frankly I am not even interested in hearing their excuse as it will no doubt make no sense.

Today women are blamed for the choices that men make to become brutal, senseless, and heartless serial killers. Anthropologist of social violence Dr. Herbert Gayle claimed his research pointed to women as the culprits who not only unleashed violence on her male child, but I would dare say also murdered his power of choice. According to Dr. Gayle, it is women, who rob men of their freewill to refuse a murder contract to shoot an innocent man, woman, or a child. However, how come the same man would be immune to pulling the trigger on himself (although he does so at times but usually after he wreaks destruction on others)? These are senseless arguments advanced by the males.

A more sensible theory could be that after sin the Y chromosome that determines the male no doubt could be called the Lucifer chromosome. However, the X of the woman chromosome teaming with the Y for the male child is man's hope to become the new man in Christ. Jesus Christ the Son of God came to Earth only through the woman to save both man and woman. The woman needed the savior just as the man. She was under serious attack from the dragon as Revelation alluded to in chapter 12 verse 13. The dragon persecuted the woman, which brought forth the man child.

We all have the power to choose. Men display wimp tendencies and need to be firmly reprimanded so they can truly evolve into the men they are designed to be. So, in summary, he senselessly invented evil, murder, deception and lies. The inventor of anything has authority over the invention. He owns the invention. The owner is HE. Satan is the owner of sin and evil.

Adam the male of the human pair, was created first. Adam, like Lucifer senselessly sinned against God therefore replicating Satan's invention in committing sin in like manner. Adam was not deceived.

Satan was not deceived yet they willfully knowingly go against God. There is consistency.

God created the woman after he created Adam. Woman, man's equal and helpmate, was created as the vessel through which the problem of sin would be solved. Joseph, Mary's espoused, was forbidden any participation in her pregnancy because the vessel could not be polluted by man. "Then said Mary unto the angel, how shall this be, seeing I know not a man? And the angel answered and said unto her, The Holy Ghost shall come upon thee, and the power of the highest shall over-shadow thee: therefore, also shall that holy thing which shall be born of thee shall be called the son of God" (Luke 1:35). The sin problem was destined to be crushed, head hook and sinker through the seed of the woman, who was to be placed in her directly by the spirit of God.

He in the triune God (Jesus Christ the son of God) stood up triumphantly to Satan who sought to challenge the rulership and authority of the Godhead. The righteous God permanently defeated sin and its author the devil.

Whosoever will, be it he or she let them come and taste and see that God is good and will save all them that come to the Godhead by Jesus Christ.

Divisions among humans, he and she will soon be uprooted, as oneness is restored, and the Earth made new. However, we still live in a sinful world wherein there is senselessness in leadership dominated by He. Man will remain at the head on Earth, as he must choose to undo his submission to Satan's authority and instead submit to God's authority. Submitting to God's authority is equality.

MY THEORY ON WHY SATAN TEMPTED EVE FIRST AND NOT ADAM

"Lucifer mysteriously allowed himself to cherish evil thoughts, and any desire, good or bad can become so strong that at the slightest opportunity one can act upon such a desire."

"And when the dragon saw that he was cast into the Earth, he persecuted the woman which brought forth the man child" (Revelation 12:13). Let us find out more.

And God said, "Let us make man in our image, after our likeness: and let them have dominion over the fish of the sea, and over the fowl of the air, and over the cattle, and over all the Earth, and over every creeping thing that creepeth upon the Earth. So, God created man in his own image, in the image of God created he him; male and female created he them. And God blessed them, and God said unto them, be fruitful and multiply, and replenish the Earth, and subdue it: and have dominion over the fish of the sea, and over the fowl of the air, and over every living thing that moveth upon the Earth" (Genesis 1:26-28).

As sin would have it, the female over the male was gifted to bear not just Earth's population in pain but to also bear the Savior of the Earth and watch him being murdered. Clearly there was a plan afoot by the dragon to destroy the woman and the church. The Godhead created the pair of Adam and Eve upright and none was more upright over the other.

The woman was not created weaker than the man, neither the reverse. They were both created a little lower than angels were as stated in Psalm 8:5 and Hebrews 2:7.

Did God create man to rule and lord over woman? No, God did not create Adam to lord over Eve and neither man today to lord over woman. Man is designated head of his household but not as a controller over his wife and children to robotize them. Man and woman were jointly in charge of the Earth as equal partners until sin intervened. Just as Satan assumed dominance of the Earth via sin, so the man has also assumed dominance over woman via sin. God gave him no such authority.

Angels are created by God and are ministering spirit beings. Man is created as Earthly human beings to minister one to the other. "Be ye kind one to another tender-hearted forgiving one another even as God for Christ's sake has forgiven you." The Bible says God will give his angels charge over us to keep us in all our ways. There is to be a relationship between spirit beings and human beings.

God is omniscient in that everything lay bare before him and he knows all his creation fully and completely even before their beginning and right up to their end. This includes spirit and human beings alike.

The Godhead speaks of the Father, Son and Holy Ghost and is referred to as he, he and he. However, do remember as clearly stated above that Genesis 1:26-28 includes the female as the male, both being creatures from the same Godhead after their likeness. The Godhead is therefore also she, she and she. It is senseless to argue otherwise. But why the he dominance? Satan's first target on Earth was the woman. He lied to deceive Eve and brutally contradicted

God. (Read Genesis 3:1-4.) But why did he pick on Eve? This question can only be answered by first having more knowledge of sin and the first sinner.

Satan formerly Lucifer was one of the heavenly spirit beings created by God. These spirit beings are called angels. Read Colossians 1:16 & 17. It was said of Lucifer, "Thou wast perfect in thy ways from the day that thou wast created". In Ezekiel 28:15, Lucifer was referred to as an angel of light and was always referred to as a he. In fact, he was called son of the morning in Isaiah 14:12.

This son of the morning and angel of light committed the first sin in heaven and on Earth. Evil, duplicity, slander, iniquity, lying, deceit, murder, every antisocial behavior first began with he. "Thou wast perfect in thy ways from the day that thou wast created, till iniquity was found in thee" (Ezekiel 28:15). "He corrupted his wisdom, and his heart was lifted up because of his beauty but he was going to be cast to the ground" (Ezekiel 27:17).

Lucifer turned himself into Satan, the dragon, the serpent, a devil, a slanderer as he was opposed to doing righteously. First, he was perfect in his thoughts and ways and he initially revered and worshiped his Creator and life giver.

However, Lucifer thought about becoming the god of heaven and god of the universe. He became intensely emotional about it and obviously felt that if it can be conceived, it can be achieved. The vain and selfish desire gradually gained ascendancy in the head and heart of Lucifer leading him to believe he actually deserved to be exalted and worshiped, especially as he began to feel great admiration for his looks and his special skill sets to sing and give council to other angels. He began to think of himself as superior to everyone else including his very life giver.

Although a spirit being, he was a beautiful spirit, he had a mind, a heart, a voice to speak and sing so don't be fooled into believing that a spirit is a mere thing. Invisible to us he is but he is almost like us. David in the Psalm told us we were made a little lower than the angels were.

Lucifer had the power of freewill as we do. He could engage such powers to break from a pattern of thought that was luring him on a course of separation from God. Equally, he had the power to continue to be passionate about such unholy thoughts.

Allan McIntyre the author of the book Parenting Criminals in an interview with the hosts of a Jamaican morning talk show program

Fresh Start said, that in one moment, you can have a decent parent and in another split moment you can have that very same decent parent becoming a devil. Moment here would speak to the fallen nature of man from the very first sin.

Lucifer mysteriously allowed himself to cherish evil thoughts and any desire, good or bad can become strong enough that at the slightest of opportunity one can act upon such desire.

A man who constantly watches child pornography is more likely to either engage in immoral sexual behavior with children or support the behavior. For those who think it their right to blame God for evil we only have ourselves to blame by the things we constantly feed into our thoughts and minds. "He that committeth sin is of the devil; for the devil sinneth from the beginning. For this purpose, the son of God was manifested, that he might destroy the works of the devil" (1 John 3:8).

"Let no man say when he is tempted, I am tempted of God; for God cannot be tempted with evil, neither tempteth he any man; but every man is tempted, when he is drawn away from his own lust, and enticed. "Then when lust hath conceived, it bringeth forth sin; and sin, when it is finished, bringeth forth death" (James 1:13-15).

"... Be ye transformed by the renewing of your minds. The mystery of iniquity doth already work" (1 Thessalonians 2:7) Satan in heaven rebelled against God and the will of the Godhead. "He that committeth sin is of the devil, for the devil sinneth from the beginning. For this purpose, the son of God was manifested, that he might destroy the works of the devil" (1 John 3:8).

The he first initiated evil, he first lied and deceived, murdered, waged war placing the he forever in the limelight from creation right up to this very day.

Sin therefore originated with Lucifer an angel created by God. Satan and his followers totaling one-third of the sons of God slandered the Godhead in heaven and were eventually cast out of heaven to Earth. Satan brought sin, evil and death to Earth as indicated in Revelation 12:7-9.

WHY DID HE PICK ON EVE? HERE IT IS.

There is absolutely no doubt in my mind that Satan with his pride and ego having influenced a third of his angelic spirit brothers to side with him against his assault on the authority of God led him into believing that it was now more important to focus on breaking down the will power of Eve the female of the human pair. He believed Adam would fall in line thereafter and he would then become lord of the Earth. Adam did fall in line without any reason, deception or pressure and proved Satan right. Satan cannot read minds, but he can use his own sinfulness to make assumptions that will prove correct from time to time.

In heaven Satan was unable to break down the willpower of the heavenly angelic daughters of God who proved to be a force to be reckoned with. Lucifer failed miserably against the angelic daughters in heaven. This hurt Lucifer's ego. David had to conquer Goliath to win the war. Lucifer also had to conquer Eve to win the war on Earth.

So, Satan became very presumptuous, and no doubt fine-tuned his reasoning that he will have to take out the most difficult target first. This was obviously based on his experience in not being able to influence even one of the daughters of God in Heaven. He also no doubt calculated that Adam his other target would be more like him and would fall in line behind Eve.

Satan set out and used a variety of deception on Eve. Satan projected himself to Eve as a god knowing good and evil and mounted a challenge against God the Creator. He would have also projected himself as a living testimony to Eve that although he ate from the forbidden tree was still very much alive knowing both good and evil. What in the world was evil? I could hear Eve questioning. If you are alive then you are not dead must have been uppermost in her mind as she was highly intelligent. Eve must have invented the saying "seeing is believing". I am inclined to believe that Satan indeed had Eve spellbound and deeply hypnotized as he in complete desperation was highly driven to hurt God and was prepared to say and do anything to get Eve to sin. It's like a desperate man in excessive heat to have sexual intercourse with a woman and is prepared to descend to rape just to "bruk" as a Rasta man declared in a video circulated some time ago on WhatsApp.

Eve became deeply trapped from too deep an engagement with the enemy and ultimately disobeyed the command of her loving God and Creator. Sad indeed!

Adam, who was then not in the least deceived, knew very well what God required of him the very moment Eve approached him with the forbidden fruit. However, senselessly just like Satan's calculated guess, Adam allowed his emotions and feelings to take preeminence over the power of reason and followed Eve his wife into transgression. It was not and is still not possible for a created being; a creature to usurp its creator and life giver. This is totally impossible and senseless.

Today, men use the same tactics on women repeatedly; the easy target being young impressionable girls. Men oftentimes lead girls into believing that they possess the sexual prowess and skills to have unprotected sexual intercourse without getting them pregnant. The young girls get trapped especially when on a couple of occasions, they may escape pregnancy but once the activity continues without the use of protection, pregnancy inevitably occurs. Below is a question-and-answer account taken from a feature called "Doctor's Advice" from the Jamaica Gleaner dated January 16, 2016.

Question: Doctor, can a girl trust guys? I am almost 17, and a virgin. Twice recently, young men have tried to persuade me to let them 'enter' me.

They both told me where it would be quite safe because they only planned to 'be inside' for a minute - and then they would pull out.

Can I believe either of them? I found it a little strange that both said the same thing. And one of them told me he was almost sterile and therefore could not get me pregnant.

Answer: Well, young guys do tend to employ broadly similar approaches when trying to persuade females to give in.

So, again and again boys will say things like:
'It wouldn't do any harm to just put it in for a minute.'
'You don't need to worry because I'll be careful.'
'It's perfectly safe because I know what I'm doing.'
'I know I just can't be a baby-father. My doctor said so.'

What you need to bear in mind is that many young males are driven by an enormously powerful urge. It is an urge, which will make them say almost anything to get into the vagina.

If a guy tells you something which is obviously intended to make you 'drop your defenses', you should just pay him no mind! Satan did the very same thing to Eve and she let down her defenses by listening to a most stupid and senseless argument that she would most definitely not die, should she separate herself from the life giver. Men thereafter seek to cast blame on the girls and will at times demand abortions or simply disappear or in some cases, murder the young girls.

On the other hand, no one can deny how easy it is for men to influence each other to do evil as seen in almost all gangs today. The term the alpha male has been coined to describe the phenomenon. That alpha male can empower other men to gang rape one female, to go on robbing sprees, to trade in guns and drugs, etc. The boys or the men's club is also a very popular phenomenon in our world today having very great influence and power over politics, money, women, and children.

It is very easy for men to agree that they should have as many women as they desire while parading that they can't help themselves in their sexual desires for women. They will be quick to tell you about King David and his son King Solomon who had many wives and concubines totally oblivious to the facts that back then such relationships did not work just as they do not work today. Men are as usual ruled by their emotions and not by listening to the voice of reason and the recorded Biblical experiences in 1 Corinthians 10:6-14 tell us to be careful not to commit the sins that were committed by our forefathers, but to shun and to take flight from all such sins that God hates. Proverbs 6:16-20 speaks to some very profound sins that God hate.

It is also very important to observe that Satan was intent on having the finger pointed at the woman accusing her of having led Adam into sin. Is that not cunning? Satan totally despised the female gender, while surely in full control of the male to do his evil biddings, a show of complete contempt for men.

Woman in the bible both means the female gender and God's church. Revelation 12:17 reads, "And the dragon was wroth with the woman, and went to make war with the remnant of her seed, which keeps the commandments of God, and have the testimony of Jesus Christ". Genesis 3:15 reads, "And I will put enmity between thee and the woman, and between thy seed and her seed; it shall bruise thy head, and thou shall bruise his heel."

The seed of the woman was the only answer to the sin problem caused by the Lucifer. Without God's plan for the woman the salvation of mankind was doomed. Satan was intent on destroying, disfiguring, and maligning the reputation of Eve or any woman to destroy Jesus the Christ, who would permanently eradicate Lucifer.

Jesus could only be born of a woman. Hence the Virgin Mary, a remnant of Eve's seed, gave birth to Jesus Christ. The seed of the woman permanently damaged Satan's head. Mary's husband Joseph could not have participated in that birth. God would not have allowed it.

He who invented and first sinned, he who ripped the Godhead apart was defeated by He who knew no sin; born of a woman.

On Earth today the he continuously invents sin. Child molestation is man's invention. Like the devil, the man points the finger at the child's mother, and the very child as the ones to be blamed for the cruel act conceived by and carried out by the man. The child is blamed for luring the man into sin. What cunning? A woman is blamed for having unprotected sex with the man and the man is then called a sperm donor.

Women are blamed for the underperformance and absence of boys in universities today. Men are often heard in the media begrudging the female university population. Adam said to God in Genesis 3:12, "And the man said, the woman whom thou gavest to be with me, she gave me of the tree, and I did eat." Men refuse to take responsibility for their sinful and cruel acts. Satan uses women and gets the men to use and discard women just as he does. Wow!

Unfortunately, women have become so lost in their responsibilities to be man's helpmate or assistant to see his folly. Instead, they become fooled and blinded by man's foolish interpretation of scripture. Man elevates his ego. He searches for exaltation and worship from women. She in turn gives him just that and becomes an apologist for him doing more harm to an already bad situation.

It was distasteful to hear one such female male apologist on a morning talk show blaming women for men's involvement in theft and murder to impress a woman and I was heartened when her guest, a male, immediately corrected her advising her that the blame is totally on the man. I must say I really did enjoy that moment. God just needs a few good men, and one would be amazed at a turning of hearts to righteousness.

A wife and husband are partners in marriage and should both honor and submit to each other as unto God or as it is fit in the Lord. Ephesians 5:21-33, Colossians 3:18 and Peter in 1 Peter 3:7 indicate that none is to act better than the other.

Submission, worship, and honor are required of both the man and the woman by God to worship and honor only God. However, after sin, man assumed and adopted dominance over woman seeing and treating woman as property and even demanding worship from her.

Eve was very deceived as she hearkened unto the voice of the serpent and not unto the voice of God. Adam in turn did not hearken unto the voice of God but unto the voice of Eve without being deceived.

Adam became subjected to Eve instead of God. God chastised Eve. She listened and hearkened to the serpent and God chastised Adam because he hearkened to the voice of Eve his wife. Man must refuse to listen and give into the voice of women luring them to commit acts of evil. The greater burden of submission was placed on Adam whose maker and ruler is God. Adam was first created, and therefore should have first listened and be instructed by God who is first and last.

Being led by God, he then becomes fit to show leadership. However, we are encouraged always to obey God rather than man. God in his foreknowledge indicated to Eve that she was going be ruled over by her husband. Paul in his epistles gave many admonitions to the wife to submit to her husband as being the head of her and the household.

I have no doubt that Paul was familiar with the male ego. Wives were to take great care to honor and love their husbands giving them every support to overcome their temper and many shortcomings, to use the seat of consciousness, the HEAD, to command a godly household. This is the reason for man being the head of his household. What better way for him to learn self-control and responsibility for his actions. Has he learned? Is he learning?

Why are men marrying children in Sudan? Why do men elsewhere in the world pass it off as culture? Why do so many households have children without fathers?

Husbands in the same spirit were admonished to love their wives as they love themselves. Husbands are encouraged to hearken to God's commands and take command of their wives as God is head of the church and the head of all things. Jesus treated women, men and children with respect and love and men ought to do likewise. Jesus never ordered any woman around during his sojourn on Earth.

Husbands and wives, males and females are reminded that, "There is neither Jew nor Greek, there is neither bond nor free, there is neither male nor female: for ye are all one in Christ Jesus" (Galatians 3:28). All have sinned and Christ died equally for all.

He from the Godhead, God's son Jesus Christ was the only and ultimate matching counters to subdue and defeat he who originates evil and sin. My theory is that if one of the angelic daughters of God in heaven had turned herself into a devil, we would be seeing the opposite of that which exists today. My theory is that she from the Godhead would assume dominance, would die for our sins and the Bible would be filled with accounts of women. However, that was not to be.

Jesus the son of the Godhead defeated Satan, mortally bruising his head forever. Jesus died in fulfillment of the wages of sin being death taking the death that should have been ours. He however completed the defeat of Satan by rising from the dead assuring us of life everlasting soon to come. Satan was evicted and was doomed forever.

All this was the reason for God warning Adam and Eve about being obedient so as not to experience death. Death became a reality when Lucifer disconnected himself from the God who is the life source. "But of the tree of knowledge of good and evil, thou shalt not eat of it; for in the day that thou eatest thereof thou shalt surely die" (Genesis 2:17).

Sin and evil and death existed before Adam and Eve fell. Therefore, Eve was not the first sinner. Lucifer was the first to sin and having won over a third of his male counterparts in heaven and failed to garner support from his angelic sisters assumed his most difficult target was Eve and so first launched his deadly attack. What do you think? Does this make sense?

"And when the dragon saw that he was cast into the Earth, he persecuted the woman which brought forth the man child" (Revelation 12:13). The man-child was however born and redeemed the world leaving us with hope for the Earth which will be made new.

Here is an interesting story that influenced my thoughts on the impact of male dominance in world leadership, frequently referenced as patriarchy. It also extends to men's involvement in violent activities and other related topics.

Balaam, formerly an Israelite prophet of God successfully influenced the Israelite people to betray God. The account took my mind back to the fall of humans. Balaam was as skillful at deception as Satan. He used a woman to assist him with his plan of deception to get Israel to disobey God. Satan used Eve out of his jealousy and envy towards God to influence Adam's betrayal. Does this give you a better understanding of the history of men using women? Balaam coveted God's position as the supreme ruler over all; Satan did similarly. Such a position and entitlement befitting God the Creator is forever beyond the reach of every creature. Balaam's artful and cunning deception to get God's people to sin was just as artful as Satan's deception in getting Eve to sin against God. Eve fell head, hook, and sinker just as the children of Israel did. Balaam was credited as a genius; however, he was a fool just as Satan was a fool to challenge God the Creator. Read about it in Numbers 22.

God cares not about how much money one has and how smart one is at devising plans to accumulate all riches and prosperity and progress. In fact, he chased an entire congregation out of church for their money dealings. No money dealings are ever equitable. God is concerned about our characters and not our power to use money as a control tool. The monetary system is primarily about money, power, control, and more money. Balaam's primary goal was acquiring gold, silver and becoming second in command to Balak. He was determined to do anything to get rich and be highly exalted. Balaam in his selfish pursuits lost everything including his life. Money is a silent weapon of mass destruction.

Government and opposition parties are like Balaam. Their masters are those who control the creation of money, and its supply represented as Baal. Some people worship either party, worshiping Baal. They all think that without money, life cannot go on. They believe their abilities to be, is dependent on money. They reason that once Baal approves of restructuring programs, everything is on track; on the right trajectory, on track to hell of course for many.

Baal's female representatives are like the pawn in the hands of their male counterparts at the top of the pyramid. Men easily lead women primarily because most women continue to believe that men are their supreme leaders and masters. Put not your trust in man or princes says the Psalmist David. We are also encouraged to obey God rather than man.

Very few females will resist or challenge orders or dominance from males. However, Queen Vashti challenged an order issued to her by her husband. When her husband the King commandeered her and her female guests, "Ladies come out and parade your bam bam before me and my men", she told him to go to hell. She would not be led on a public display of leg, breast, and thigh before he and his drunken party of men.

Balaam used a woman to influence the younger women in Israel to flaunt themselves to the Israelite men, getting them, all sexually riled up and you know what happens to men when they watch porn, etc. Flesh takes over.

Patriarchy today, continues to rule contrary to God's desire for peoples to make informed choices. "My people are destroyed for lack of knowledge." Patriarchy espouses donmanship and elevates lack. Patriarchy ensures that love for God and love for each other remain at odds. Many people continue the path to destruction for LACK OF KNOWLEDGE fueled by lack of money.

MEN AND VIOLENCE

Men have a most important role to play in eliminating the widespread problem of violence in our world today. The solution clearly must start somewhere and what better and more profound place to start than at the head.

Violence in our society today is mostly attributed to men. Statistics show that males perpetuate most violent acts in Jamaica and males are the main victims of violence. Statistics also show the gun as the weapon of choice in the committal of acts of violence.

Many have proffered fatherlessness in the homes as the main cause to this phenomenon, even as the news reports are bombarded with accounts of men raining violent attacks against women, children, the elderly and other men.

Sexual violence is very popular on the list of violent attacks. Oftentimes sexual violence leads to murder and suicide. Oftentimes the rest of society describes the offences as senseless and indeed, it is just that.

The origin of violence is rooted in senselessness, totally devoid of reasoning. If reasoning was to be engaged and applied, many problems could be solved using nonviolent means.

Earth's first violent encounter was between two males, which resulted in murder. It is recorded as follows, "And Cain talked with Abel his brother: and it came to pass, when they were in the field, that Cain rose up against Abel his brother, and slew him" (Genesis 4:8).

Violence is deeply rooted in deception and must be further examined. The record of the world's first deceiver is documented in Genesis 3:1-4. The World's first deceiver is referred to as a he named

Lucifer albeit a spirit being but with the mindset of a man to do evil. He is also called the serpent and the Dragon.

Ezekiel 28:15-16 and Isaiah 14:12-16 zero in on the origin of violence, deception, iniquity, sin, and evil all pointing to Lucifer as the inventor. "Thou wast perfect in thy ways from the day that thou wast created, 'till iniquity was found in thee. By the multitude of thy merchandise, they have filled the midst of thee with violence, and thou hast sinned." Verse 16 of Isaiah 14 reads, "They that see thee shall narrowly look upon thee, and consider thee, saying, is this the man that made the Earth to tremble, that did shake kingdoms?" Satan brought sin and violence to Earth. Genesis 2:17, Romans 5:12, Revelation 12:9 & 13.

On the contrary, another man named Jesus Christ, God incarnate, opposed violence, and brought peace and love to a violent Earth. Deuteronomy 32:4 speaks to the perfectness of God's work for all. "His ways are judgment; a God of truth and without iniquity, just and right is he." Job 34:10 states, "Therefore hearken unto me, ye men of understanding: far be it from God, that he should do wickedness: and from the Almighty that he should commit iniquity."

God created a human pair, (human beings) male and female. Male is designated he and female she. Genesis 2:21 identifies male as he and the woman as she in Genesis 2:22-23. God created man in his own image, male and female. It is very accurate to refer both man and a woman as man or men. However, he always means male and she female. Eve the first female transgressed, and her husband Adam followed her and transgressed. Adam cast the blame for his transgression on his wife Eve.

Blaming others for your mistakes and using others to cover wrongdoing are serious acts of violence. Violence began with the human pair. Lucifer transgressed against God in heaven then blamed God for being selfish, causing his transgression. As it was in heaven, so it is in Earth.

Lucifer the first he spirit being had no cause to sin, was not deceived yet he sinned against God his maker. Adam the first human, he had no cause to sin was not deceived but nonetheless sinned against God his maker. Eve the woman, was deceived by Lucifer. Lucifer used the serpent to do evil against Eve. In other words, he ganged upon Eve. Eve approached her husband alone. Deception and usury are acts of violence. God in his foreknowledge and wisdom therefore first laid out what would become the problem, which was characterized by the senseless choice made by Adam. The precedent was already set in the heaven with Lucifer who similarly made a senseless choice to sin.

God provided the solution in his Son Jesus Christ, born of a woman to permanently eradicate the he who started evil both in heaven and on Earth against the woman. "And I will put enmity between thee and the woman, and between thy seed and her seed; it shall bruise thy head, and thou shalt bruise his heel." Eve although created the same day as Adam was created after Adam. There began the solution to the problem started by the he. Jesus the savior was to be born of a woman whom Satan was intent on destroying.

The male descendants of Cain were a huge problem as seen in Genesis 6. Sexual immoralities saw the men treating women with disdain taking as many wives as it pleased them, and violence became the order of the day. Today, men formulate themselves in gangs and do similarly and in the process also create many jezebels who support them head hook and sinker.

In Sodom, the men again were caught up with pride, sexual orgies and idleness which led to mayhem and violence. God could have only found one man in Noah's time and one man from the city of Sodom and Gomorrah who he could work with to restore some semblance of order.

Abraham, Moses, Aaron, Joseph, David and so many other men received overwhelming attention and test from God in the building of their characters to prepare them for positions of leadership against violence. The Bible is filled with the account of men receiving endless attention as the problem of violence escalated one king after the other. Kings after kings after kings ruled, some dreadfully evil while a few others subjected their reign to God's leading. Is there a government today that subjects its leadership to God's leading?

Jesus' sojourn on Earth over two thousand years ago saw him recruiting and focusing primarily on men from all backgrounds and educational standing. They required special treatment in the building of their characters, so they could learn how to lead effectively in problem solving on many issues including the problem of violence.

It is therefore obvious that men have a most important part to play in the solution to the problem they started; hence the man must be the head. Do men today know this? The solution must clearly start somewhere and what better and more profound a place to start than at the head. The head is where the seat of consciousness lies. God set the precedent where the focus must be. But the relevant focus is lacking in our societies today. Men do as they please. Today's men are consistently waging violence and sexual immoralities on women, children, other men, against countries and are in many instances they are lightly reprimanded. Men's explanations for such acts of violence receive endorsements from numerous other men and an increasing female support, escalating the crisis. How similar is man's behavior to that of his mentor Lucifer?

Imagine a being becoming so deceived into believing that he could successfully attack the very one who gave him life?

This I must say is the most outrageous of all deceptions and hence totally senseless. Such was also a form of deception that contains a type of emotion and feeling of being superior, which was rooted in physical beauty as related in Psalm 10:4, Ezekiel 28:17 and Ezekiel 16: 15.

It is also significant to note, how Satan used violence against Job, a man from the land of Uz, one who feared God, claiming that God built a hedge around him. Notwithstanding that, God similarly had built "a hedge" around Satan when he was Lucifer the angel of light in Heaven. What the Lord blessed Job with paled in comparison to the many blessings God bestowed Lucifer. No one assaulted Lucifer with any acts of violence as Satan did to Job and his family. No one took away Satan's beauty, but he laced Job with skin sores. No one took away Satan's amazing ability to sing four and possible more harmonies at once. Yet Satan sinned against the one who made him and then had the audacity to accuse God of protecting Job to justify his accusation against Job of serving God simply because God provided for him. Yet Satan's deception is so smooth, full of cunning, that today, many people readily side with the devil in blaming God for allowing evil to afflict Job without cause, while ignoring the fact that without cause, Satan sinned and waged war against God in heaven. Job, then having much cause from physical sufferings and loss of his children, servants, and properties, did not curse God but rather stood up for God. Lucifer on the other hand had no reason to curse God, but he cursed God anyway. Is this not a justifiable condemnation against Satan? Can you pinpoint similar levels of crazy deception, ingratitude, and violent acts on Earth today? Satan's attack on God was always an attack on God's right to be God of all creation.

The Bible says in the beginning God, and not in the beginning Lucifer or Satan. Satan first created divisions in heaven as he created the first army of men who were other sons of God, to join with him in a vain fight to be independent of God and to rule the heavens.

The first violent war was fought in heaven and Satan lost. However, Satan was successful in creating the first war in the human pair.

Today, under men's rule on Earth from the beginning of deception until now, women have been assigned the position of weaklings. This worsened under a man by the name of Charles Darwin who in his Darwinian theory that the survival of the fittest and the strongest is the normal way of life in the affairs of men. Men are ignorant of their role as head, believing headship to be lord overall, trampling upon the weak and being totally oblivious to the voice of reason for the demonstration of character in their dealings with women, children, and the elderly. "It is certainly not by might nor power but by character", found in Zechariah 4:6.

Jesus while as a man on Earth served mankind. Mark 6:56 and Luke 19:5, 6 give the account. Jesus came to Earth to show men how to be real men. Children had no fear of him. Women had no fear of him. Other men had no fear of him as he was compassionate and warm to all. Read about his love and compassion in Mark 10:13-16 and John 4: 9, 27. Jesus treated women with dignity. He was humble. He washed the feet of other men as a humble servant. He was sensitive to the needs of others. He healed all who came to him and did not abuse them. He was sensitive and always displayed self-control in some of the most difficult and trying encounters with other men. Read Peter's record in 1 Peter 2:23. He did not try to or harm or be violent to those who opposed him.

In war, the male soldiers oftentimes rape women and children. The Boko Haram Islamist group from Nigeria captured and enslaved hundreds of schoolgirls. In Sudan, men prey on children even 8 years old, marrying and molesting them. In Jamaica, men also prey on children, women, and the elderly. Men prey on children, women, and the elderly who they describe as weak in all countries across the world.

Ellen G. White in her book The Desire of Ages says, "Lucifer desired God's power but not his character." It always takes character to care for the weak and again weakness is man's invention not God's creation.

Satan lost the war against God miserably. He also lost miserably the war against the daughters of God in heaven. Satan has a hatred for God just as he has a hatred for women, and for sure, he desperately hates men as he uses them for their physical strength, beauty, and poor reasoning abilities to unleash violence. Violence is anti-social and senseless, and suggests deep mental illness rooted in fear, false pride, very low self-esteem, and devil possession.

After the fall of the human pair God who is omniscient, told Eve in Genesis 3:16 that Adam will rule over her. This was directly because of sin coupled with the fact that Adam believed and blamed Eve for his sin. It's the same today as men blame women for sin and evil and ruling over them.

Man's behavior then and now is not a surprise to God. Neither was Satan's behavior a surprise to God. Males like Satan believe they have superior leadership qualities and they have every right to rule the world and will do just about anything to rule. Males are primarily driven by ego and pride, two very dangerous emotions. Please note that God's divine plan for humans, male and female is for equality, collaboration and oneness in occupying and having dominion or care over the space on Earth given to all by the Creator. Because the male craves power, he will engage in war, competition, and divisions (divide and rule) to manipulate and control others. This aspiration directly opposes equality and oneness, opposing God and good. Anyone who opposes God supports the devil.

Cain took on the character of Satan when he slew his brother Abel, then chastised the Creator when asked to give an account of his brother "Am I my brother's keeper, or am I to love my neighbor as myself?" Cain rudely asked God. Siding with the devil is opening doors to discord and abnormal relationships. Satan's rulership is only based on evil, independence from God/apostasy, blame gaming, lies, deceptions and duplicities.

Man, further went on to commit the first polygamous relationship when Lamech decided he wanted more than one woman for wife found in Genesis 4:19. This was a decision taken solely and exclusively by man and has no foundation in God's divine order. The violence resulting from such deviation from God's original plan for intimate relationship between just two has been pronounced throughout Biblical recordings. Men have been very cunning in their teachings throughout history that they have entitlement to many females. They use the Bible inaccurately to support such utter foolishness. David, Solomon, Lamech and all the men in the Bible who had more than one wife were manifesting Satan's character of greed and utter selfishness. Greed and utter selfishness are usually devoid of reasoning and always result in violent, antisocial behavior and ultimately death. Just read below and see.

David had many wives and still coveted Bathsheba, Uriah's wife and orchestrated his murder. David introduced the first known "jacket" child concept in his time by urging on Uriah to sleep with his wife to pass off his child onto Uriah. God then asked Nathan to reveal David's sin to David who immediately not knowing the guilt was on him was in a hurry to commit another violent act of murder. Read about it in 11 Samuel chapters 11 and 12. This was a clear indictment on David because he immediately knew such an act was sinful and would not have desired such on himself, yet he was committing sin against his brother. Wife stealing and murder will only bring more of the same. Today we call it trading, cheating, giving bun and psychologists reason it away by saying it's the hormonal effects and the biological make up of man. Look at the reaction of men when they cheat versus when their wives or girlfriends cheat. The stupidity and senselessness of it all is that the man cheats on his wife with another woman who is the wife or girlfriend of another man, his very brother. There is no applied reasoning, no brain power, or the use of the HEAD by those assuming headship.

Lovers of pleasure not lovers of God hold prominence. The boyfriend or husband who becomes so intoxicated with the sexual pleasures from his partner oftentimes kills his lover for suspected cheating then kills himself. Imagine the elimination of hurt and violence should a man stop to reason before murdering his wife or girlfriend whom he suspects is cheating. This has been made worse by his worship of money. Men are most angry when they have spent money on a woman who then cheats with another man. A man having money is a man with power and whoever he spends it on becomes his property. He will therefore be most angry if his power over his property is benefiting another man and he is therefore more likely to kill his cheating partner. He and the rest of society will highlight the money spent by the man whether to assist with the education of the woman or to provide her with a place to live, etc. He and his societal supporters will not reason that money is never more important or of greater value than the life of a human being.

How can they when they have all been fed the notorious lie that it takes cash to care? They will not even apply basic reasoning that the man got more than his money's worth. He got his big favorite, SEX, which was what he was really buying. He got brawta in having his food cooked, clothes washed and pressed, children looked after, domestic help overall. However, there is nothing to him like his money, and being woefully obsessed with the thought that he has lost all the money he spent on the woman, he must resort to violence to satisfy his inflated ego and pride. His love and worship of money also exceeds the importance of the vagina. How so? A man will pay a prostitute for sex and after he satisfies himself will rob her the very money he paid for the sex.

Imagine the elimination of hurt and violence should men also stop to apply reason before sexually indulging children up to 17 years old? There is absolutely no applied reasoning but pure raw emotions. Man cannot eliminate sin and the consequences of sin in our world today. However, men have the power and authority through Christ to get rid of quite a lot of the damages done by himself in sinning against each other and God as well as to ease the sufferings in the world. Matthew 5:44-48 instructs us to love and forgive. Luke 10:29-37 teaches us to be neighborly to each other. Philippians 2:1-8 encourages us to be humble as Jesus was. Will men temper their egos and pride recognizing that their systems of ruling the affairs of men and women especially today with all their technological innovations will never bring about peace and prosperity to Earthlings?

Will man as the representative of the human pair turn to the Creator Jehovah God for guidance to lead, realizing that his tendency to be violent can only be solved in Jesus?

Will man call upon God for guidance and directions as Matthew 4:4 admonish to live and rule according to the word of God or, will he continue to rule violently?

Come on guys, you have so much strength, stop wasting away and start loving. Love is of God. God just need a few good men and the few will translate to many. What a world it would be! The end shall come.

SEXUALITY

I noted that homosexuals are fearless in coming out to say they are gay risking being separated from friends, families even losing their life; in essence being subjected to endless ridicule. Heterosexuals then label gays as sick, insane, reprobate people on Earth and even worse. I thought that for gays to publicly come out about such alleged insanity demonstrates defiance, some honesty, and no doubt some rare courage. Imagine not caring if the masses ridicule you, ostracize you or even possibly kill you? However, telling me you are gay will cause me to make informed decisions; for example, I would not be inclined to leave my teenage son unsupervised in your company.

On the other hand, I would also not be leaving my daughter in the company of a heterosexual male who although a child molester, would never so declare his preferences and like a thief in the night would be making out with my child or his stepchild or even his own daughter for as long as he can without getting caught. Even when caught he would deny and lie endlessly. It is written in the scriptures in John 3:20-21 that, "Everyone who does evil hates the light, and will not come out into the light for fear that their deeds will be exposed. But whoever lives by the truth comes into the light, so that it may be seen plainly that what they have done has been done in the sight of God"

I thought about many of the sexual abuses committed by heterosexual pastors, teachers, so called law-abiding people who are cited as trustworthy. I questioned, "Where is their rare honesty and courage? Today, many heterosexuals are rapists and child molesters. Many are kidnappers, human traffickers selling children and body parts in exchange for money. They are indeed sick, insane reprobates on Earth. Should they have the honesty, rare courage, and defiance of the gays, to declare their preferences, millions of girls, women, and boys could be spared the physical and psychological trauma meted out by these hypocrites. There are facts in the same Bible which clearly states neither heterosexuals nor homosexuals are esteemed one above the other, because God hates every sin large or small. Lying lips are also an abomination to the Lord and so is child molestation that God declared it were better a millstone be hung around the neck of the offender. The esteemed of God are those who love God, love fellowmen, and do God's will.

Ezekiel speaks to the abominations of Sodom as pride, fullness of bread, abundance of idleness, neglect of the poor and needy as reasons for their fiery fate. Heterosexuals use the Bible to ridicule homosexuals that it appears sexual immorality is only homosexuality. But look at Leviticus 20:1-27 in the Bible from which the reference is extracted. Here, God was advising Moses to inform the children of Israel of their fate, should they commit whoredom with a profane image-worshipping group of Molech people.

Today, we are not all Israelites by nationality but all God's chosen people by adoption as declared by Paul in Galatians 4:4-5. Is it still applicable to uphold such requirements? Is there still a Molech group among modern day Israelites? 1 Corinthians 10:6 reads, "Now these things were our examples, to the intent we should not lust after evil things, as they also lusted." 11 Timothy 3:16-17 offers further clarity, "All scripture is given by inspiration of God, and is profitable for doctrine, for reproof, for correction, for instruction in righteousness: that the man of God may be perfect, thoroughly furnished unto all good works.

The recorded behaviors in Leviticus that displeased God and for which death should be the punishment are as follows:

Israel interbreeding with Molech, an evil and whoring system; the breeders should be killed. This would mean that heterosexuals should be killed once they had sexual relations with the ungodly idol worshipping Molech people. Did heterosexuals overlook this fact?

The Israelites who knew the offenders and refused to put them to death should also be killed. Again, this does not exclude heterosexuals.

1. Those who seek out and practice witchcraft should be killed.
2. Those who curse their mothers and fathers should be killed. Let us note the 3rd., sin speaks to sexual intercourse between heterosexual men and women, which reads.
3. Those who commit adultery with another man's wife, his neighbor's wife, the adulterer, and the adulteress both should be put to death. Does adultery occur among homosexuals?
4. Any man sleeping with his daughter-in-law, both offenders should be killed.
5. A man who lies with another man should be killed.
6. A woman who lies with another woman should be killed.
7. A man sleeping with his wife's mother should be burnt with fire.
8. A man who lies with an animal; both man and animal be killed.
9. A woman who lies with an animal, both woman and animal be killed.
10. A man who sleeps with his sister should be killed.

11. A man who lies with a woman during her period should be killed.
12. A man sleeping with any of his near relatives, all should be killed. This is incest and is very common today among heterosexuals.

Let us look at Proverbs 6:16-19 which speaks to six sins that God hates and the seventh sin which is an abomination to the Lord. Are these sins common among both heterosexuals and homosexuals?

1. A proud look
2. A lying tongue
3. Hands that shed innocent blood
4. Heart that plans wickedness
5. Feet that love to run into mischief
6. A false witness

The seventh is being a troublemaker who sets up people against other people. Wow! How many of those mischief makers do you know today? It seems to me that heterosexuals who set up mischief against homosexuals would be committing abomination.

Proverbs 6:29, clearly states that a man who engages in sexual intercourse with the wife of his neighbor is an adulterer and is not innocent even if he touches her. It seems to me here that if he should be killed, it would not displease God as sin number three states that he hates the hands that shed innocent blood and therefore there would not be a violation as the man and woman would not be innocent and therefore can be killed. Is that also your understanding? Why therefore aren't adulterers sought out and killed today?

Let us move on to Romans 1:18-32 and continue our probe into sins that are punishable by death.

1. Ungodliness
2. An unrighteous man or unrighteous people
3. An idolater, who is a person worshipping other men, four-footed beasts, money, birds, jobs, images, etc.
4. Men and women going against nature sleeping with each other
5. Fornicators, which is sex outside of marriage
6. Covetous people, which is "red eye" for another person's property

7. Malicious people, which is a destructive behavior towards others and their property

8. Bad mind and envious people. (Ask the Jamaica dancehall musicians about the bad mind they sing about in their lyrical chants in almost every other song they release. Ask them as well if they could name you the bad-minded people they love to chant about.)

9. Murderers

10. Deceitful people

11. Whisperers

12. Backbiters who are people full of pride like those who love to proclaim that they are a proud homosexual, a proud heterosexual, or a proud child molester.

13. Inventors of evil

14. Disobedient to parents

15. Covenant breakers

16. Unmerciful. Ask some Jamaicans from what is termed "inner-city communities" about their sons with hands on their heads pleading for mercy on their lives to our local policemen and women who would just get deaf and release the gun's trigger to pierce its bullets into the bodies of the victims.

Romans 1:32 says all such people are worthy of death. Should all such people be killed, who would be left alive today? Wait. Also, in 1 Corinthians 6:9-10 fornicators, idolaters, adulterers, abusers such as child molesters, thieves, drunkards, and extortionists are reprobates.

Galatians 5:19-21 continues the naming of adultery, fornication, uncleanness, lasciviousness, idolatry, witchcraft, hatred, variance, emulations, wrath, strife, sedition, heresy, envy, murder, drunkenness and reveling as sins worthy of death. They that do these things shall not inherit the kingdom of God. If one will not inherit the Kingdom of God, which other kingdom is there to inherit? In addition, why is the sin of adultery and fornication so repetitive throughout the Bible?

1 Corinthians 5:11 admonishes us not to keep company with fornicators, idolaters, drunkards, and extortionists. Read Galatians 6:26-28 and Psalm 11:5 for further clarity.

1 Timothy 5:8 refers to heterosexuals who bring children into the world and then abandon them or abandon their family; they are worse than an infidel.

An infidel is one who does not believe in the Creator, who does not believe in God. It appears that if a homosexual believes in God, he stands a better chance to heed the word of God over a heterosexual who denounces God or visa versa. Nevertheless, it is a terrible sin to procreate and then abandon the family.

Revelation 22:14, 5 seem to be pointing to men who refer to themselves as old dogs whose mission it is to have as many women as they can. They are described as whoremongers and liars. The Bible has clearly spoken and not the author of this publication.

I categorically refuse to be judgmental of my fellow humans especially realizing that I should have long died from my indulgence in several of the sins written about. In fact, Romans 2:1-3 warns me not to be judgmental of others. 1 Corinthians 4:5 also reads, "Judge nothing before the time, until the Lord come, who both will bring to light the hidden things of darkness and will make manifest the councils of the hearts: and then shall every man have praise of God." Matthew 7:1-5 gives us hope whether heterosexuals or homosexuals.

Nonetheless, the question should be asked: By what and whose authority are common-law relationships (fornicators or an unmarried couple living together for many years) elevated to the same status as marriage, and accepted as a moral, legal heterosexual union? Is it not elevated to such esteemed status simply to ensure that all the parties involved will get material/monetary benefits should a member from the common-law group become deceased, especially if the union produced children? Are homosexuals lobbying for a similar elevation? They, having been denied benefits to property owned by their partners have further elevated their relationships to marriage status to derive all the benefits that come with such a status? Is this not money hoax and money being a silent weapon of mass destruction?

Heterosexuals have clearly ignored the Bible's stance on fornicators but not homosexuality, preferring one sin above the other. Satan is certainly succeeding in using one sin that incensed heterosexuals to the point where they lovingly embrace sins on the quiet side such as adultery, incest, fornication, drunkenness, smoking, sexual promiscuity, common law relationships and murder. What cunning?

How many heterosexuals openly express their pleasure at the shooting death of 49 alleged gay people at the nightclub in Orlando, Florida, USA in June 2016? Many, who hate not just the act of homosexuality but also those involved in the act, believed it was a direct punishment from God. Is it true that a Christian pastor told his congregation from the precincts of the pulpit that the gays got what they deserved? It appears he finally came out of his closet as a murderer.

Do you know how many other thousands, millions possibly of heterosexuals who quietly find the shooting murder of the 49 ecstatic? Did you know that they are equally murderers like the pastor but of the secretive type? Do you also know that to rejoice in the killing of your neighbor is the manifestation of hatred?

The same Bible speaks, "He that loveth not his brother abideth in death. Whosoever hateth his brother is a murderer: and ye know that no murderer hath eternal life abiding in him" (1 John 3:15). "If a man says, I love God, and hateth his brother, he is a liar: for he that loveth not his brother whom he hath seen, how can he love God whom he hath not seen? And this commandment have we from him, that he who loveth God loves his brother" (1 John 4:20-21).

Did you know that heterosexuals elevate condom use as a substitute for love? They say love, protect and respect. They also say use a condom every time. Such are clearly lovers of pleasures more than lovers of God. Homosexuals no doubt do the same. Listen to the 'use a condom advertisement' with the well-loved and respected artiste Freddy McGregor. He says that a condom is even more important to use with a strange partner. This is direct prostitution being encouraged in a subtle way. Do you recall what the fate of whoremongers should be?

Again, heterosexuals are pleasured by the fate of the cities of Sodom and Gomorrah in Genesis 19. Heterosexuals claim that it was the sin of homosexuality, which kindled God's wrath to rain fire and brimstone.

However, Ezekiel the prophet speaks to the abominations of Sodom as pride, fullness of bread, abundance of idleness and neglect of the poor and needy as reasons for their fiery fate. An abundance of idleness and fullness of bread would surely breed sexual immoralities. Working people and I mean people doing REAL WORK would surely have no time for the sins of sexual immoralities common among mankind then and now. Walk around

Earth today and you become stunned by the amount of work to be done. However, a great majority of the Earth's population is unemployed and this is made worse by the fact that many who claim to be employed are in the sporting and entertainment industries earning billions, empowering them to draw more crowds of males and females for even more sexual immoralities and inequalities of the worst kinds using their huge income base.

Did you also know that sexual immoralities among heterosexuals are recorded in Genesis 6 in the Holy Bible where God also destroyed an entire world save Noah and his family? Heterosexual men took as many women as they pleased, and I am inclined to believe that sexual orgies were popular among heterosexuals just as it was among homosexuals in Sodom and is today among both groups. Men have a strong tendency to operate sexually in groups and gang rape. Genesis 19:4, 5, 11 and Genesis 6:2 record for our learning. Can you imagine the horror that women back then suffered at the hands of heterosexual men? And this has been so right down to the time when Jesus walked this Earth. Can you recall the story of how a group of heterosexual men took a woman they claimed they caught in the act of adultery to Jesus? My theory is that those very men were the ones who committed adultery with that woman hence when Jesus wrote their sins in the sand, they all disappeared leaving her alone with the one who could pardon and give her the new life she was obviously in need of.

The wickedness and evil of heterosexual men and women were so grievous to God that he destroyed an entire world of men, women, children, animals, and plants. You do know of the story of Noah and the Ark, don't you? Jeremiah 23:14 also speaks to adultery, walking in lies, strengthening the hands of evildoers as grievous sins of Sodom and Gomorrah and Jerusalem; they were present in the days of Noah and they are similarly grievous sins in our world today.

Lord, please be merciful unto us sinners and forgive us our sins as we forgive others. Help us to seek to do good and to think and do good to others and to do the things which are honest, pure, just, and holy. Help us to show our love to you as we show love, mercy, and compassion to our fellowmen. Amen. To God be the Glory!! Read John 3:15, Psalm 15:1-5, Galatians 5:22-23, Galatians 6:1-10 and Romans 12:1-21. They sure make beautiful reading. Do not stop reading now!

Here is more hope. In Galatians 5:22-25 we are told; "But the fruit of the spirit is love, joy, peace, longsuffering, gentleness, goodness, faith, meekness, temperance: against such there is no law. And they that are Christ's have crucified the flesh with the affection of lusts, if we live in the spirit; let us also walk in the spirit."

Now here is the best part. Ezekiel 18:21-32 reads, "But if the wicked will turn from all his sins that he hath committed, and keep all my statutes, and do that which is lawful and right, he shall surely live, he shall not die. All his transgressions that he has committed, they shall not be mentioned unto him: in his righteousness that he hath done he shall live.

Have I any pleasure at all that the wicked should die? Saith the Lord God: and not that he should return from his ways and live?

But when the righteous turneth away from his righteousness, and commiteth iniquity, and doeth according to all the abominations that the wicked man doeth, shall he live? All his righteousness that he has done shall not be mentioned: in his trespass that he hath trespassed, and in his sin that he hath sinned, in them shall he die.

The way of the Lord is not equal. Hear now O house of Israel; is not my way equal? Are not your ways unequal?

When a righteous man turneth away from his righteousness and committeth iniquity, and dieth in them: for his iniquity that he hath done shall he die.

Again, when the wicked man turneth away from his wickedness that he hath committeth, and doeth that which is lawful and right, he shall save his soul alive.

Because he considereth, and turneth away from all his transgressions that he hath committed, he shall surely live, he shall not die.

Yet saith the house of Israel, the way of the Lord is not equal. 0 house of Israel, are not my ways equal? Are not your ways unequal?

Therefore, I will judge you, 0 house of Israel, everyone according to his ways, saith the Lord God. Repent, and turn yourselves from all your transgressions; so, iniquity shall not be your ruin.

Cast away from you all your transgressions, whereby ye have transgressed; and make you a new heart and a new spirit: for why will ye die, 0 house of Israel?

For I have no pleasure in the death of him that dieth, saith the Lord God: wherefore turn yourselves, and live ye." This is applicable to both homosexuals and heterosexuals.

We can turn away from evil if we truly desire to love God and love our fellowmen. The reward is eternal life. I want that, how about you?

Can a heterosexual or homosexual person choose Christianity, but knowingly rejects or accepts one, more than one, or all the following beliefs, and still be an exemplary Christian, ardently believing that he or she will inherit God's Kingdom?

- Rejects Jesus Christ as being God Divine
- Rejects Baptism by immersion
- Rejects Baptism in Jesus' name only
- Rejects Baptism in the name of the Father, Son and Holy Ghost only
- Rejects that you must speak in an unknown tongue to be saved
- Rejects the 7th day Sabbath as one of the Ten Commandments to be kept forever
- Rejects the giving of blood to save a person's life even the life of a close family member
- Rejects being sorry for the violent murder of homosexuals or heterosexuals, child molesters and murderers
- Rejects forgiving a neighbor for committing the sin of adultery with their partner
- Rejects the administering of care to any homosexual or heterosexual AIDS victim
- Rejects that a homosexual can become a Christian or can ever be saved
- Rejects that the eating of pork and all other foods rendered as unclean for human consumption found in the Holy Scriptures is still relevant
- Rejects that Christmas and Easter are pagan holidays and should not be commemorated

Are you competent to answer the questions? Do you personally know Christians who believe all 13? How many do you believe?

Finally, although initially I did not deal with the point that homosexuality is branded by heterosexuals as a terrible wrong on the basis that two men or two women cannot procreate (have children), I wish to say:

God created sexual intercourse for the purpose of procreating. How so? Simply by asking the following question: "If God did not design sexual intercourse for procreating, why use contraceptives during or after the sexual act which in essence prevents or terminates a pregnancy?"

There is never a concern for contraceptives between two males or two females, except maybe to prevent the spread of infections but NEVER TO PREVENT A PREGNANCY.

Sexual intercourse does not occur between two males or two females if one accepts that sexual intercourse was created for procreation, which it is. The point made by heterosexuals would therefore be of no worth.

The blame for putting brakes or stopping the continuation of humanity can never be placed at the feet of homosexuals. Such blame can only be placed at the feet of heterosexuals who were created to continue the Earth's population. All sexually active heterosexuals who use contraceptives or abortion, consciously decide to put a stop on peopling the Earth; not homosexuals who are not so gifted.

Sexual intercourse is a built-up activity to ultimately climax. Climaxing or experiencing an orgasm creates pleasure and results in procreation. To not climax especially for the male causes' disappointment and pain. Clearly disappointment and pain are not pleasurable for anyone.

In an interview, a friend gave me his account on sexual intercourse as follows; "It would really be frustrating to enter a sweet vagina and be forced to pull out before cumming. I would be quite upset. I have had occasions when I have sex and didn't cum, but that was because I had too many ejaculations before and therefore there was nothing left to cum. Those have been very frustrating occurrences."

This is the fact:

It is the ultimate release of semen/sperm from the male referenced as "a cum" that provides pleasure for him. Without the release of semen there is no fulfillment, satisfaction, or pleasure. Without the release of semen into the vagina of the female there can equally be no procreation or pregnancy occurring.

Conclusion on this point: sexual intercourse is created for procreation and procreating is pleasurable. One cannot exist without the other. What you choose to do with the semen or the pleasure, whether to give it life or discard it, is your choice, a choice only heterosexuals have. Homosexuals have no such choice.

Carrying a child into this world should be done from a position of prior planning. It is a continuous debate driven with passion, energy and hype on the rights or wrongs of a woman exercising control over her body and aborting her unwanted pregnancy. Many favors the acts while perhaps an equal number abhor it. Legislation, which criminalizes abortion, has long been in existence in Jamaica and other countries. Many are asking that it be revised to accommodate abortion of the fetus for incest, rape, and a threat to the life of the mother. Others will have none of it.

In my opinion, the passion, energy, and hype need to focus in areas where it really matters. Together, let us discover where the focus should resonate to better impact lives.

In looking at the design and creation of planet Earth including its contents, its cycles, and the creation of the first human pair, there is no doubt in my mind and probably yours, that they were not created by accident, neither from an act of carelessness nor by force. In fact, the Earth and all that is within it, testifies to deep thought, freedom of will and a deliberate decisive manifestation of such thoughts by its Creator. It is also obvious that the Creator ensured the Earth was first prepared or made fit to sustain the first human pair he deliberately and methodically gave life. Therefore, it is my opinion that, so it is to be with humans in procreating, as we are God's thoughts made audible in Earth. Under our current capitalistic form of running the Earth, it is even more important for people to responsibly and thoughtfully plan before they create or extend their families.

We should create and procreate from a sense of thoughtfulness, utilizing freewill responsibly, and with a consciousness that fully embrace the value of caring for and sustaining a life brought into this world of capitalism.

Currently, if a man uses brute force against a woman and gets her pregnant, he is fully supported by the law of the land, to compel her to have the child, totally against her will. Should she exercise her freewill to abort the unwanted pregnancy and is caught, she would be prosecuted under the law as a criminal having committed a murder. How preposterous? God is the sole judge of every woman who decides to utilize their freewill over their own bodies. In my opinion the circumstances of rape, incest or to save the life of a woman are most unusual circumstances. A woman's body is indeed the temple of God and a man has no right to defile it. If it is defiled by incest, rape, or any unwanted sexual intercourse it is the woman's right to rid her body of whatever will result from such defilement, period. If carrying the fetus to term is an imminent threat to the life of the mother, she has a right to choose her life over that of the fetus. We should allow God to apply and execute his own judgment according to his will and in his own time. How dare any human to put him/herself in the place of God? The prophet Jeremiah made this submission; "I the Lord, search the heart, I try the reins, even to give every man according to his ways, and according to the fruit of his doings" (Jeremiah 17:10). God alone can search hearts, read motives and intents from every possible perspective.

Anyone objecting to a safe/lawful termination consistent with the treatment for defilement and bringing down God's wrath on women, should be answered and dealt with according to their folly lest they be wise in their own conceits. What is being implied by these fools is that God must have instructed this demon-possessed man to break not just God's laws but that of the state by raping a woman to get her pregnant; or instructed a father to sexually molest his own daughter even lying to her that it's normal, or to molest his niece or grandchild as if to say his sperm will know that they are related, hence there will be no conception.

Sperm is not partial and once discharged in any fertile womb will result in conception of a fetus. We as responsible adults must ensure that if such a sperm is transmitted where it is not wanted, such as being thrust upon a child, an unwilling adult, from one family member to another, then we must undertake to safely terminate its further work of maturing into an unwanted child, especially when the woman is totally unwilling to have her body be used as a carrier.

I am fully aware that we are imperfect people living in an imperfect world. So, many people will at times become careless and oblivious to ideals of thoughtfulness, prior planning in consensual moments of sexual arousal and gratification. Some might have utilized contraceptive methods, however, because this can fail, an unplanned pregnancy can result. A woman therefore has the right to accept or reject the pregnancy. There also exists, incidences where a woman is told the pregnancy must be terminated to save her life. She also has the right to terminate the pregnancy and preserve her life.

A woman might decide to carry a pregnancy that resulted from the undesirable and careless act of rape. One might label her careless not to have exercised her rights over her body and aborted the pregnancy that was forced on her. Assuming she was inept in being a good parent as is the case of many mothers and fathers in Jamaica today, her inability to provide for and educate that child unfortunately resulted in the creation of another demon-possessed individual who has become a part of one of the many criminal gangs in Jamaica or elsewhere. The irony is that while she would not have been called a murderer by anti-abortion groups and would not have a running with the law of the state for keeping the pregnancy, at no time did the anti-abortionists or the state feel it was their responsibility to intervene and offer her assistance in the rearing of her unplanned child. So, because of her impoverished circumstances, she became derelict in her responsibility as a parent, which over the years resulted in the creation of a child that she, the state, its military agencies, and anti-abortionists are now at pains to rid the society. Oh, how they appear on political platforms and in the media calling down hellfire and judgment on the various criminal gang members, robbing, raping, and taking thousands of innocent lives. Many want them dead and if they don't do it themselves, will rejoice when it is done by the state's military. What mixed up values.

Some women have managed to use an unplanned or unwanted pregnancy thrust upon them as their wake-up call to turning their lives around for better; hence they have the child then moved ahead onto a relatively stable life. Others have not managed as shown earlier. However, others chose to manage the imperfection by taking the decision to terminate based on their individual circumstances. Sadly, however because abortion has been legislated as a criminal act with severe penalties, many who have taken that route have had to deal with adverse health issues and even death because they had botched abortions to escape being criminalized by the law of the land.

By using legislation to force a woman against exercising her right over her own body, in choosing to responsibly terminate an unwanted pregnancy that she might have possibly acquired by force, accident or carelessness is tantamount to tampering with a woman's freewill given to her by her Creator, and any such tampering is to be fully rejected. Those who lobbied for the legislation to prohibit the rights of a woman, those who enacted same, and those who are again lobbying for its stay, are not only lacking in character as the devil is lacking in character, but they, like the demon-possessed men that force themselves onto a woman or child are altogether worse than the devil himself. Somehow, I am also reminded of a period in history where runaway slaves were hunted down not to be the beneficiary of a free life but for their hunters to be handsomely rewarded with money and the slaves returned to a life of miserable enslavement.

I am yet to see evidence that the Creator or the devil forcefully demands worship from any human being. Although we were created by God, which means he owns us, he did not make us submissive robots to his every bidding. The devil tempts people to submit to his evil will. We have the freedom of choice to yield to the devil or not to yield. The Creator encourages people to use their freewill to accept God's gift of salvation. Yet again, we can choose to yield or not to yield. Jesus said, "Choose you this day whom you will serve." Therefore, a state that uses legislation to deny a woman the right to have a safe abortion as a way out of ridding herself of an unplanned pregnancy thrust upon her whether via rape, incest, or the failure of contraception is tantamount to enslaving the individual.

A woman's freewill and dignity should never be tampered with by anyone as it relates to her effort to consciously position or reposition her life to her suit. The chicken always comes before the egg and therefore the woman is free to exercise her freewill over her own body and all that it contains. This is by no means suggesting a lack of a possible further engagement. Albeit she might have already made up her mind from her own reasoned perspective to abort the pregnancy. But, because it is possible that she might have also experienced pressure from the father and others, warning her to terminate or not to terminate or else face cruel consequences, additional engagement with an experienced and unbiased professional(s) should always be a part of the package offered at the proposed established safe abortion facilities.

Legally safe abortions should be allowed for:

1. The rape of a woman that forces on her an unwanted pregnancy
2. The sexual abuse of a child
3. Incest

4. Failure of the contraceptive method engaged, resulting in a pregnancy the woman does not want
5. Freaky immoral sexual acts among idlers or prostitutes; clearly with the primary aim being sheer pleasure or perhaps sex for monetary gains, but no desire for procreating.

Nevertheless, if a woman desires to exercise her freewill to carry the pregnancy to full term, she should not be scorned or denied assistance by those who oppose but be supported especially in areas of nutrition and employment opportunities. Don't ever forget that a woman is entitled to exercise her God given freewill.

No doubt, some women who have had children from being sexually abused or raped are pleased with the outcome of their decision not to terminate the pregnancy. On the contrary, others are also very happy they chose abortion even without any forced acts of abuse. Their choice makes them no less a person or deserving of a criminal sentence. Who are we to reject, discriminate and judge? We should always be willing and ready to offer full support out of respect for individuals who decide to terminate or not, regardless the circumstances under which the pregnancy occurs.

As a matter of policy, anti-abortion groups should be encouraged to volunteer themselves and their time to bring financial, social, physical, and emotional support and stability to the parent and the child conceived via abuse, incest, or rape. In fact, it should be their joy so to do, and if they protest or refuse to lend support, then I suggest they shut up.

A decision to terminate should also be viewed as a personal decision like the decision of worship and vote, and therefore the state, its agencies and non-government organizations (NGOs) should in no way impose or tamper with a woman's freewill to abort her unwanted fetus. An individual should be allowed the dignity to worship God or not, to vote for his party of choice or not to vote. It would be better to prohibit or criminalize people who maliciously and deliberately permeate public air spaces with the disgusting smell from the smoking of cigarettes, tobacco, ganja or the consistent burning of garbage in backyards. Such commonplace activities negatively impact air quality and the lungs of unborn fetuses that women choose to bear and include millions of people in general, leading to ill health and untimely death. Such occurrences assassinate our freewill to breathe clean air. I view all smokers as deliberately suicidal and malicious, possessing intent to murder and no doubt many have committed many murders.

The healthy development of fetuses always gets lost in the power hungry, attention seeking anti-abortion groups whose primary desires are for sheer manipulation and control of women who responsibly decide against birthing which is their God given right so to do. Their focus would be better spent to ensure that fetuses kept and carried to full term are spared the assaults of smoke pollution by selfish and irresponsible men and women.

The points below are worth pondering, in recognition of the fact that freewill or the freedom to choose is an individual entitlement given by God to everyone and a fetus carried to full term may or may not support abortion even when they were so spared. They too will exercise their own freewill, choosing what they perceive as best for themselves.

Doctor V's mother was a victim of rape. She had planned to abort the fetus. However, she listened to many arguments for and against and finally took a decision to have the child. Her son grows up, becomes a doctor, supports abortion, and in fact has aborted many pregnancies. Vigorous protests against abortion will not influence an unborn fetus to abhor or favor acts of abortion. Worthy of consideration too, is the fact that a woman who chose to terminate is of no threat to the health, safety, and life of countless others in the exercise of her God given freewill to abort responsibly. This is important bearing in mind the next point.

Cigarettes, an evil creation in my opinion, are manufactured in billions with absolutely no sanctions from any 'anti group' to criminalize manufacturers or their customers. Millions of smokers utilize their freewill irresponsibly to smoke whenever it pleases them. Such choice is obnoxious; it debilitates the health, safety, and life of even countless unborn fetuses as well as the lives of millions of non-smokers. Such deliberate irresponsible exercise of freewill also adversely affects the health and wellbeing of the very smoker. Is the attention seeking anti-abortion groups willing to criminalize men and women who can easily be classified as slow and deliberate murderers of unborn fetuses, non-smokers and even themselves? How about topping their fame by taking on cigarettes and smokers of ganja who create a "hand-middle rubbing disease" found in every nook and cranny of the globe? Is it possible that the backlash anti--abortion people would encounter from smokers and the manufacturers and suppliers of cigarettes and weed, might have them wishing they could instantly abort grown up fetuses? Here are people who have exercised their freedom of choice with absolutely no care that they are violating the freedom of others to breathe in God's fresh air and to choose not to smoke.

One should not disregard the woman's choice not to inhale the unwanted smoke deliberately imposed upon her and her unborn fetus, yet anti-- abortionists do and further think it's their right to tell her she cannot choose to terminate her unwanted pregnancy that would also be exposed to ill-health and other developmental hazards.

Judge A's mother: a victim of rape is quite proud of her daughter's achievements. She is against abortion. However, her daughter having presided over cases of brutal rape and incest where in some instance's victims were severely abused and some murdered, is in support of abortion from rape and incest, much to the disappointment of her mother. Again, vigorous protests against abortion will not even influence an unborn fetus to abhor or support the act.

Solomon in Ecclesiastes 4:1-3 speaks to the experiences of the many people who are so terribly oppressed, and although others had power to spare them such oppression, they offered no comfort. Solomon even went on to say that he praised those that were already dead rather than those who were alive and experiencing the onslaughts of evil. He said, "Had those who were alive not been, they would have been spared such trauma." Clearly, if they were not born or conceived, they could not have experienced such brutal trauma and evil. One is not born if there is an abortion. One is also not conceived or born if contraception is used before or after the sexual act. The unborn cannot therefore be burdened with evil.

It is however quite clear that capitalists value capital over human beings. Capitalists accumulate wealth from both safe and unsafe/botched abortions. They accumulate wealth from after-sex abortion pills, and they accumulate countless wealth from all forms of contraceptives that are used daily by billions of people. Are manmade contraceptives not unnaturally developed products which ensure man can derive only half of the fun from sexual intercourse; not the complete fun, which is procreating as intended by God? In Genesis 38, I read that a man successfully used perhaps what could be described as the natural contraceptive method, sending it to the floor when it was supposed to have been used to fertilize an egg. Was that the death of a fertile live sperm?

Nonetheless, abortion should be made safe by legislation. Indeed, capitalism and cash still win either way.

Some members of anti-abortion groups embrace capital punishment. Is taking a fully-grown life okay over aborting a fetus? It's like saying the doctor whose mother had wished to abort but was stopped, should now be executed, or charged for manslaughter because he has become a murderer by performing abortions. Do anti-abortionist groups in Jamaica go after doctors?

I am aware that varying stages of a pregnancy can be life threatening to the mother who may have decided to terminate not knowing the associated risks. Indeed, all surgical procedures are risky and as such it is the general practice of medical professionals to advise patients of the associated risks from surgeries and ensure they accept full responsibility for the outcome.

It is not relevant in the least that the unborn fetus might be the next president, a judge, or a doctor. It could very well be a child molester and a murderer. No one knows, therefore this ought not to be used as an argument against legalizing abortion. No one knows beyond the shadow of a doubt the likely outcome for anyone. However, the woman knows she wants a termination of her unplanned pregnancy and should be allowed safe medical courtesies. She has a choice and should not be criminalized for deciding to abort her accident or a pregnancy that was brutally forced upon her via rape or incest.

Likewise, the argument that life is sacred and precious is indeed applicable and pregnancies should be planned and conceived in love in a marriage. It is highly unlikely that abortion would be considered under such circumstances unless the mother's life is at risk due to complications. However, should victims of rape and incest choose to have their babies, it is their freewill so to do and such lives beyond the shadow of a doubt are also sacred and precious. Unfortunately, many such lives become subjected to indignities.

It could be easily argued that the unwanted 13-year-old child currently on the streets of Kingston could become the next president. The 14-year-old child who was raped and murdered could have had a great future too. But who bothered to care? Who knew? No one, as it appears once the child is birthed, quality of life is of no importance to many capitalists. An increase in the number to capitalists means more profit. Quality of life is always important and should be the number one priority among leaders and advocates. Attention to providing quality of life for men and women would in my opinion lessen the incidences of rape, incest and other sexual abuse usually stemming from idleness, illiteracy, homelessness, landlessness, overcrowding in some homes, poor infrastructure, joblessness, inferior healthcare, all having their genesis in a lack of resources or lack of cash. It is terribly unfortunate that the majority are led to believe it takes lifeless cash to care.

What do we know? We know the children have been here for 13 and 14 years respectively. We know they need care and protection.

We have the known right in front our very eyes every day crying out for attention on the streets of the city of Kingston and every parish in Jamaica and around the world, and we are in parliament and everywhere in the media arguing about the unknown. At times when they come up to our cars, to ask for cash to buy food to temporarily ease the hunger they are feeling, we turn our windows up, and chase them away. I see them; you see them too and they need urgent care and guidance.

You anti-abortionists and capitalists wanted them here and what are you doing now that they are here? Is it that you have no cash to care? And how will you find the cash to care for the additional fetuses you want carried to full term babies?

We also do know many pockets are enlarged by several billion-dollar orders for security cameras, guns, ammunitions, motor vehicles, speed boats, helicopters and many other crime fighting tools and implements to be used to reign in the unwanted children who have taken on a lifestyle of crime and violence due to lack of care and attention from those fighting against abortion.

We know the 13 and 14-year-old children who are placed in homes and boot camps are at times severely beaten and abused physically and sexually. Do capitalists frequently visit them, provide foster care, educate, and train them in life skills? You have no cash. Is that not your excuse?

We do not have fetuses begging on the streets and being beaten and denied the basic life sustaining necessities. Instead, we have children and young adolescents in very overcrowded homes being molested by their own relatives. They are even molested by people in high leadership positions and members of advocacy groups who they claim give them money and food in exchange for sexual favors.

Pharisees you are, wasting precious time, energy, and money over unborn fetuses.

It is quite a contradiction to be marching against rape, incest, sexual abuse and the murder of women and children, while vigorously supporting the birthing of fetuses from rape, incest, and sexual abuse to the point of making criminals out of women who choose to terminate such pregnancies. Carrying these pregnancies to full term many times is like bringing more children into an already miserable abusive situation oftentimes perpetuating the cycle of abuse. Forcing a woman to have a child she rejects, forces her to do an illegal abortion, which can impact her health in the long term. Should she not terminate, her built-up resentment over time will contribute to an unstable child with mental/psychological imbalances.

Again, capitalists don't mind as this means another opportunity for making more money. They run races and set up fancy foundations collecting millions and making big announcements of giving help to some struggling hospitals to aid some mentally and emotionally disturbed children of poverty-stricken mothers and fathers. Of course, a few will survive, as the monetary system must thrive.

Where is the advocacy to change the cycle of abuse to a cycle of thoughtful and careful family planning? Where is the advocacy for quality education for all, for all to find and live their God given life's purpose, which is to be in good health and prosper? Leave the unwanted pregnancies dead. Advocate for protection and care for the now living unwanted pregnancies right in our very faces; boys and girls in children's homes and others homeless on the streets. Legislate and act for their welfare and good life. They are here. They are now and are the future of the country. If a woman takes the decision to abort an unwanted pregnancy, support her in law.

I warn, if we don't, we will only be supporting more botched abortions that complicate the health of thousands of women or be repeating the cycle of unwanted pregnancies roaming the streets as beggars, prostitutes and criminals living a miserable, short, unfulfilled life in wait of a terrible death.

Oh, but misery is what fuels the system of capitalism because the more one can create adversities the more one can capitalize on the misery utilizing money or the lack thereof to cause more misery to the majority but furnishing wealth to a few.

Money is placed on a pedestal as the solution to all human problems, yet there is never enough of it to help humans out of their problems, hence both botched and safe illegal abortions will continue indefinitely.

WHAT DO MEN THINK ABOUT PLANTING SEEDS?

Question: Why do you plant a seed?
Answer: For growth, to bear fruit, to produce food, for shade, for beauty and more.
Question: Under what conditions do you plant a seed?
Answer: The soil and environment must be fertile, right season for planting and
Question: What are some of the things you are required to do to make sure the soil or area to be planted is fertile?
Answer: Get as much history or background information as possible on the area mapped out for planting and
Question: If you are to achieve growth from the planting of that seed what are some of the things you must do after you have finished planting?
Answer: Water the seed as often as required, visit the place of planting as often as is possible to ensure it is thriving.
Question: Do you at any time plant a seed in fertile soil at the right season but have no interest in the growth of that seed?
Answer: (your response)
Question: If you have no interest in the growth of that seed, why do you insist on planting it in fertile soil and at the right season?
Answer: (your response)
Question: Does such an activity make any sense to you?
Answer: (your response)
Question: Can anyone get real pleasure from planting a seed he has no interest in growing or bearing fruit?
Answer: (your response)
Question: Would you at the very least be willing to stop to reason that if you have no interest in planting a seed in fertile soil for growth then you ought always to consider the following?
Don't bother to plant any seed at all or cover the seed properly with plastic before you plant it in the soil as the plastic covering will prevent the seed from germinating. Plant the seed in an infertile or dead soil.

Answer: (your response)
Question: Does it sound like a pleasurable activity to plant in dead soil?
 Answer: (your response)
Question: Does this tell you that a seed should be planted only if one wishes for growth.
To ensure growth you will also do the necessary research required for growth.
You will take every care to ensure that such growth is achieved?
You will plant the seed in the right season?
You will gladly accept the fruits, the shade, the food, etc., resulting from the planting of such seed?
You will want to know that your seed remains prosperous? Do these sound-like pleasurable activities?
Answer: (your response)
Question: If one continues to plant seeds simultaneously in season and out of season, will such not result in very little or no time at all to ensure the growth and survival of the seeds that are planted in season?
Answer: (your response)
Question: Are not such activities counterproductive and at times tantamount to confusion, madness, and senselessness?
Answer: (your response)
Question: Here is an utterance from two male radio personalities a day after Fathers' Day in June 2015: They uttered that God gives to woman the greatest thing on Earth; the thing that motivates men, and she must know how to use it to motivate the man.
Question: How many men in Jamaica do you think would agree with such utterances?
Answer: (your response) Motivational speakers preach self-motivation.
Question: Does the man possess anything to motivate himself?
Answer: (your response)
Question: Does sexual intercourse really motivate men?
Answer: (your response)
Question: Name some of the things that men are motivated to do after having sexual intercourse with a woman?
Answer: Taking care of her and the children she bears him?
Question: Are the sentiments expressed above shared and executed by 90% of men?

Answer: (your response)
Question: What are the primary or basic needs of the women involved in the sexual intercourse, the children who are offspring and of course the very man?
Answer: The woman desires pleasure too but is seldom pleasured. The woman, the children and the man need a healthy environment, a home, piped water, food, shelter, clothing, education. How many are provided with same?
Question: How many men are in Jamaica today?
Answer: (your response)
Question: How many men in Jamaica today get sex from just one woman?
Answer: (your response)
 Question: How many get sex from more than one woman?
Answer: (your response)
Question: How many of the women who have motivated the man or men are having their basic needs and the needs of their children met for food, a home, piped water, clothing, and education?
Answer: (your response)
Question: Why are so many men, women, and children in Jamaica without water, healthy food, clothing, nice homes to live in and a good education?
Answer: (your response)
Question: Does sex really motivate men to act responsibly or provide wealth for his sex mates or his many children?
Answer: (your response)
Question: What are the real motivations that men derive from having sexual intercourse?
Answer: (your response)
 Question: As far as you know or have read, was Adam, Earth's first man
created from sexual intercourse?
Answer: (your response)
Question: Does this information put to rest the senseless question about whether the chicken comes first or the egg? In other words, was it not that Adam was created first, then he reproduced? Likewise, the chicken was first created then laid the eggs or reproduced after.
Answer: (your response)

Question: As far as you know, were angels who are ministering spirit are
beings, created from sexual intercourse?
Answer: (your response)
Question: The Bible says that man was created a little lower than the angels in heaven (Hebrews 2:7). As far as you know and have read anywhere do you think angels were created with the ability to pro-create, and if so, can you provide any well researched credible evidence?
Answer: (your response)
Question: In the new Earth after the second coming of God, does the text Matthew 22:30 from the Bible suggest to you that there will be sexual intercourse taking place in the new Earth?
Answer: (your response)
Question: How important is sexual intercourse outside of procreating?
Answer: (your response)

PART 7: WHAT IS GOOD?

What is good?

God is good.

God created good.

He created good things by using thoughts and action. God exercised his freewill only for good.

"And God said, let there be light and there was light" (Genesis 1:3). After six days of creating good, God uttered that it was good.

What did God create that was good? He created day, night, atmospheric heaven, starry heavens, oceans, seas, and other large bodies of water with thousands of life forms, dry land with trees, grass, herbs, creeping things, flying creatures, cattle, and thousands of other life forms.

Then God created man (male and female) to oversee the good things he created on the Earth. Man was also created good in God's image and likeness. Finally, God created a day for rest and called it the 7th day Sabbath and that was just as good.

Man was to take care of and organize the Earth for the good of Earth's entire families. The success of this no doubt would entirely be dependent on the active participation of all the Earth's families.

George Bernard Shaw an Irish socialist, dramatist and critic said, "There is only one sort of genuine socialism, the democratic sort, by which I mean the organization of society for the benefit of the whole people."

Working in collaboration for the benefit of the whole is good.

WHAT IS EVIL?

What was created good could obviously be used to create evil. Again, it could not be done without thought and action.

Before the creation of Earth, spirit beings or heavenly creatures were also created good by God. They were created with freewill and given creative powers so they could in turn create good by using thoughts and action.

God created the Earth. He then created human beings to live on planet Earth. The human beings were also created with freewill and not as robots. They could therefore utilize their gift of choice to create good or bad.

God will not alter freewill as God changes not.

Lucifer, a spirit being, decided to use his freewill to create the opposite of good. Lucifer freely used his thoughts and action to oppose God. In doing this, he created the opposite of good which is bad. Bad is described as evil. Lucifer also created the opposite of life, which is death because of disobedience.

Lucifer utilized thoughts and actions in creating just as God utilized thoughts and actions. However, God created good while Lucifer created evil. While one-third of other spirit beings created by God, exercised their freewill and opposed good, two thirds exercised their freewill in support of good. So, Lucifer is without excuse.

Lucifer used deception borne out of thoughts and actions to deceive Eve the first of the two human beings created on Earth. He told Eve the woman that evil would yield better results than good. He sought to demonstrate by using trickery, which resulted in her switching loyalties from her own Creator to Lucifer another creature. She believed his lie that separation from God could not yield death and this was the first lie ever told.

So, we humans today are also without excuse just like our fore-parents and the ministering spirit beings, because we all used our freewill to create and support evil instead of good.

Satan continued to contradict God and has told countless of other lies since then to all his followers, and followers of God. A great majority of Earth's people still believe his lies. This also bears out in many examples of our governments and churches coming together, changing God's eternal laws, and deceiving almost an entire world of people.

God said that in the sweat of thy face shalt man eat bread, however man says not so God. In the sweat of man's face or by no sweat at all, man will first earn the money we created which he will then use to buy back the very bread that some will labor for.

God encourages us to seek his help to make choices that can be for the good of all. No, it's not easy, because selfishness abounds and the adversary, the inventor of sin/evil or the opposer of God and everything good, is still at large working through men and women to influence polices and decisions to infuse them with biases so they create divisions, fake scarcities, desperations, and built-up anger to push us to hurt each other, then blame it on God. The aim of Satan is to divide and rule. He has met with great success as he influences and uses the various political systems and parties in world governments to do just that; divide the people and rule them.

The monetary system is a most divisive world system. Money is used as the tool to create scarcities and cause people to fight each other for the so- called limited resources for their survival, and anyone who tells a nation that it takes money to care is a liar and an agent of Satan. This is evil and sadly; most people believe and live this miserable lie every day.

It is evil beyond imagination that world governments continue to force all people, nations, kindred, and tongues to use money to buy what God has freely created for our survival on Earth.

Governments or their agents will reinforce how essential water is for life, while in the same breath they will inform us indirectly that the system they designed cannot allow for the creation of and supply of said money to allow all to pay for and receive an uninterrupted supply of the very life-sustaining water. This is evil and not good.

Today, many in the world blames Eve for the sin problem in our world. However, a greater majority blame God. In fact, many profess that evil was originally created by God. This is as senseless as sin is. Many refuses to accept their responsibility in choosing evil over good. Very few blames Satan for the creation of evil. Very few blames Adam. They remain willfully ignorant; angered by evil and yet refusing to investigate its origin and the plan of action to eradicate it.

Lucifer continues to use human beings especially the ones easiest to use to continue his work of deceiving the whole world. Look around you. It's not difficult to see which creature engages in the worst of criminal activities defying all the senses. Which creature created taxation and the evil monetary system? Which creature was able to convince the whole world that it takes cash to care? Which creature commits the most senseless killings? Which creature is designated the number or mark of the beast?

Money as we know and use it today is totally rooted in evil and ripples every other conceivable evil. The love of money is the root of all evil because money is created by man and elevated as the only thing needed to acquire all that man needs for his survival including the most basic of man's need; food, water, and air, without which man dies. God created food, air, and water. Man created money. Man says you need what he creates to buy what God created for all.

WHY DO GOVERNMENTS AND THE PEOPLE CHOOSE EVIL OVER GOOD?

On March 12, 2018, teachers in Jamaica went on sick-out because the government of the day was opposed to doing one good in raising their salaries by a percentage that they thought would lessen their monetary stresses. The government feared that doing one good would mean having to multiply the good across the board for all other public sector workers. Therefore, doing good for one group would be setting a bad precedent for the others to use as an example for having their demands for salary increases met.

Jeremiah 4:22 says, "For my people is foolish, they have not known me; they are Sottish children, and they have none understanding they are wise to do evil, but to do good they have no knowledge".

When the opposing party forms the government, they do likewise. The perpetual excuse is that to do good would derail some other so-called gain or good that was accomplished and would set back the country. How can good set back a country?

I don't know the gains that are continuously referred to by both parties. Jeremiah 13:23 says, "Can the E-thi-o-pi-an change his skin, or the leopard his spots? Then may he also do good, that are accustomed to do evil".

QUESTION: Government, is there something wrong with doing good?

ANSWER: Yes, there is something wrong with doing good. If I do one good, I will have to multiply it and if I continue doing good and better, then everything will become so good that everyone will in essence thrive almost on equal terms and I will lose my stronghold of power. Such is also not the nature, or the characteristics of our monetary run economy set by slave masters under the express order of Satan who hates God. A monetary run economy at the root is a master running the lives of slaves; a continuation of slavery; not physical slavery as it was abolished, but economic slavery. Economic slavery uses money to manipulate and control humans and humans are mere laborers.

To do one good will also mean having to compromise the same good by doing an act of evil such as raising taxes to do the very good. We therefore cannot really do good.

For emphasis, a monetary run economy is not an economy that is driven by doing acts of good. In fact, it is driven by doing acts of evil multiplied perpetually.

Ecclesiastes 8:8-11 says, "All this I have seen, and applied my heart unto every work that is done under the sun: there is a time wherein one-man ruleth over another to his own hurt. And I saw the wicked buried, who had come and gone from the place of the holy, and they were forgotten in the city where they had so done this is also vanity. Because sentence against an evil work is not executed speedily, therefore the hearts of the sons of men is fully set in them to do evil."

He that knoweth to do good and doeth it not, to him it is a sin. What is Ethics?

Ethics as defined by Roget's New Millennium Thesaurus; First Edition (v 1. 3.1) is the formal study of morality.

From time immemorial, morals or morality has had its ancestral base in religious laws, which are descriptive systems of do's and don'ts given for mankind to follow as a mark of obedience, and to prevent chaos and social unrest among mankind. This system of rules from the Christian's perspective is manifested in the law as given to Moses by God in the writings of the Ten Commandments as stated in the Holy Bible. However, if Commandment 6 which reads, "Thou shalt not kill" is to be taken at face value, it would entirely rule out the now common acceptance that killing another human in self-defense is totally acceptable.

Abortion, also labeled as killing a fetus, presents another set of arguments where some pregnancies are labeled unwanted, and therefore it is advanced that a woman should be allowed to terminate her unwanted pregnancy. Here, ethics probes whether it is morally right or wrong to kill under any circumstances. Ethics also probes the scant regard for laws and the legality of said laws. Ethics seeks to probe what ought to be.

Of note, is that throughout history there has been a disturbing pattern in the formation of laws and a lack of compliance with the said laws. I have observed the following nuances in manmade laws:

• Discriminations and forced dogmas,

- Lack of enforcement of said laws,
- Breaches of human rights,
- Lack sincerity at the very formations,
- Deliberately formed to frustrate, oppress, and eliminate via competitions.

Therefore, compliance with said laws is fraught with contentious issues. For example, laws formulated in the early centuries have commanded and forced citizens to abandon their freewill and bow down in worship to another human being, a stature, or some other object. The penalty for breaking such laws could land the lawbreaker into the claws of a lion or into a fire to be burned alive.

Currently in Jamaica, we have laws that give adults what I consider access to engage in immoral sexual activities with16-year-old children. Another law prohibits the same16-year-old child from participating in the act of voting into leadership, perhaps the very man who engages her mind, body, and emotions in illicit sex. Still another law prohibits the same 16- year-old from acquiring a license to drive a car and study at a university.

What happens when a man breaks the law by engaging in sexual activities with a child of 14 years old and gets her pregnant? This is what happens. Another Jamaica law that prohibits abortion would then take effect even in instances where other illegal offences of incest or rape were committed. Such law would force that child to carry a pregnancy she was not at the age to plan for and did not wish to carry to full term. These laws cancel out the right of a woman to utilize her freedom of choice to exercise control over her own body. This prohibition has negative ethical implications.

More laws are then made beyond the capacity of the lawmakers to enforce said laws due to lack of money to create opportunities for training of personnel to carry out enforcement of said laws. Is this Catch 22?

So, for example, regulations will be created requiring developers to construct buildings according to specific building codes such as inclusion of a fire escape in a three-story apartment complex. If a developer ignores the code, the primary complaints will be a lack of enforcement and lenient penalties prescribed for breaches. The excuse often tendered for the lack of enforcement is the lack of adequately trained personnel and resources to carry out enforcement activities. The excuses for not applying penalties are that penalties are too harsh or not harsh enough, and the matter of prescribing penalties presents its own set of challenges. Nonetheless, these deficiencies are incubators for continued breach of regulations resulting in innumerable contentions and long-running arguments and counter arguments. During the contentions there are also lacks in structural integrity, environmental hazards presented by the location of the buildings, as well as building set-back breaches that oftentimes set off fierce legal battles among neighbors.

Some laws contain discriminatory languages such as laws that promoted slavery while others might not use discriminatory languages. However, enforcers are handpicked to flout said law and discriminate against citizens based on race, class, and status.

Governments also breach their own regulations from time to time, especially in their efforts and haste to gain popularity to win elections. For example, areas of the country earmarked by governments for windfall developments might first require critical studies such as an environmental impact assessment or analysis. However, the government will ignore its own regulations; bypass the required analysis and forge ahead with the development, especially when so-called record employment will result. Citizens are always in need of work and money and will happily vote for jobs to earn cash even if it means the destruction of some parts of the environment. Does it seem unethical to choose money over protecting the very environment that sustains our lives. Is this a case of the eviction of ethics?

In Ecclesiastes 7:29, the wise man Solomon declared thus, "Lo this only have I found, that God hath made man upright; but they have sought out many inventions." Solomon also said that having applied his heart to knowledge he has found out that one-man ruleth over another to his own hurt Man having great pomp, pride, and a superior air of arrogance, figures he has all rights to rule and manage the Earth's resources and its people in whatever way he chooses, and without supreme guidance and direction. He therefore sets out to manipulate and control as much as he can, to have an edge above his fellowman and uses legislations as a cover. Is it unethical to have such morally disturbed people carrying out the weighty responsibilities of running or leading a country? How does one reconcile the plan of action by potential leaders as they lambast corruption and promise a transparent government when they are rallying votes to be elected, but within months of being elected, engage in similar corrupt practices? How many times and in how many elections will they tender their plans to repair farm roads, having agreed that farming is most critical to the country's growth and development, but years would go by and the poor condition of these roads remain the number one complaint from farmers?

Making jobs available for young people, in recognition of the need to keep them out of gangs and trouble is usually another hot campaign promise, but job opportunities remain extremely scarce even after the new government is elected. While there are no direct laws against poverty, potential leaders would emotionally declare their love for the poor and their intentions to bring down poverty through progress and prosperity on the campaign trail. Where is the progress and prosperity?

This is further proof that manmade laws and empty promises are incubators for contentions and bear out from this insightful statement made by the prophet Jeremiah in Jeremiah 10:23; "O Lord, I know that the way of man is not in himself: it is not in man that walketh to direct his steps." Hence, we are always faced with moral and ethical dilemmas. Man's desire to dominate one over the other, to stifle consciences, to force dogmas, instead of collaborating one with the other in solving problems for the benefit of common good, sets the stage for continuous hostilities.

A most significant dilemma is manifested where some individuals, and in particular whites, and in recent times "brown folks", believing themselves most fit to rule the world, have strategically positioned themselves not just as rulers, but as supreme owners of key resources on Earth. Job had this to say: "Therefore they say unto God, depart from us; for we desire not the knowledge of thy ways. What is the Almighty, that we should serve Him? And what profit should we have if we pray unto Him?" (Job 21:14, 15).

Both self-proclaimed and elected rulers take command of the Earth's resources and deny most citizens equal rights of access to even basic life- sustaining resources on Earth. They are called kings of the Earth as presented in Matthew 17:25. He saith, "Yes." And when he was come into the house, Jesus prevented him saying, "What thinkest thou, Simon? Of whom do the kings of the Earth take custom or tribute? Of their own children, or of strangers?" They have also been referred to as pharaoh, one- man don, dictator, slave master, king and priest, taskmaster, the big man, the illuminati, the invisible government and by other names.

Theodore Roosevelt, 26th United States president had this to say: "Behind the ostensible government sits enthroned an invisible government owing no allegiance and acknowledging no responsibility to the people. To destroy this invisible government, to befoul the unholy alliance between corrupt business and corrupt politics is the first task and statesmanship of the day." Earth's rightful creator and owner is God. God created Earth for all humans, nations, kindred, tongues, and peoples. David the Psalmist was quite convinced on the matter and stated, in Psalm 89:11; "The heavens are thine; the Earth also is thine: as for the world and the fullness thereof, thou hast founded them." Isaiah, a servant of God also stated in Isaiah 45:18; "For thus saith the Lord that created the heavens; God himself that formed the Earth and made it; he hath established it, he created it not in vain, he formed it to be inhabited: I am the Lord and there is none else." We are here and we inhabit the Earth. In Genesis 1:28, the Creator told our fore parents to be fruitful and multiply and fill up the Earth with many peoples. Jeremiah 10:12 declares, "He hath made the Earth by his power, he hath established the world by his wisdom, and hath stretched out the heavens by his discretion."

The apostle John in John 12:31 recorded words uttered by Earth's Creator about Lucifer's temporary conquest of the Earth and his casting out of heaven to Earth; "Now is the judgment of this world, now shall the prince of this world be cast out." Paul in 11 Corinthians 4:4 speaks to Satan's influence on human beings on Earth, "In whom the god of this world hath blinded the minds of them which believe not, lest the light of the glorious gospel of Christ, who is the image of God, should shine unto them." David and the apostle Luke corroborated their stories on mankind's choice to digress from God and truth, to force his own fellowmen to do likewise and their eventual plot to destroy God's elect in Psalms 2:2-3 and Acts 4:26, "The kings of the Earth set themselves, and the rulers take counsel together, against the Lord, and against his anointed, saying, let us break their bands asunder, and cast away their chords from us. The kings of the Earth stood up, and the rulers were gathered together against the Lord and against his Christ."

Mankind's redemption was fulfilled 2,000 years ago, and despite Satan's continued sojourn on Earth a while longer, we ought not to ignore and become so blinded by the fact that God indeed defeated Satan. We must also be reminded of the fact that God desires us to also live healthy and prosperous lives during our remaining time here on Earth.

TAXATION

Centuries ago, a system of taxation was introduced and declared by one powerful ruler on Earth as the ideal economic model to manage the Earth. This has substantially created moral and ethical dilemmas for Earth's inhabitants. The system was in full effect when God fulfilled his plan of redemption by sending his son Jesus the Christ to Earth. "And it came to pass in those days, that there went out a decree from Caesar Augustus, that all the world should be taxed" (Luke 2:1).

The system of taxation primarily generates large pools of money, which is extracted from the income of citizens, or from the sale of products internally and externally, or from movements of people, etc. This money is to be used for educational endeavors, construction of public thoroughfares, provision of public transportation systems, provision of public health facilities, etc. The system of taxation has found resonance among all leaders throughout the many world civilizations. However, I have noted with much interest that for as long as the taxation system exists, the most basic needs of most of the people on Earth have not been and will never be met, for example clean safe water supply. Water is available in abundance and is needed by every human being, plant, and animal. However, it requires treatment and reliable transport to people's homes and other places of need. Taxing people billions of dollars for centuries has not resulted in a safe water supply system for all. This is because money does not work but people do, and therefore once labor is engaged many problems can be solved. The taxation system is useless in meeting people's needs. However, the handlers skillfully trap people into believing that it is a shortfall in tax collections that halts attempt to upgrade the water distribution systems. In fact, shortfall in tax collections is attributed to poor road infrastructure, poor healthcare system, the absence of necessary tools in schools to enhance learning, etc. All this is simply to justify the need to borrow money from those who claim exclusive money manufacturing rights. This is a very neat arrangement for power and control over people and resources.

Nevertheless, while there is clear evidence of an abundance of work, and corresponding evidence of an abundance of people needing work coupled with the abundance of available material to accomplish work, but taxation and money is advanced as the only solution for work And, those who have assumed authority are always able to convince citizens that:

- Monetary resources are lacking to mobilize work,
- They require money to purchase the necessary material and to pay for labor
- People are lacking in the required skill and expertise to do the work

No one bothers to ask whether it is a bad thing for people to benefit from good and therefore do governments have the right to withhold good from the people by using a lack of money tag line as an excuse?

I have observed with keen interest that both the material and monetary needs of those offering such lame excuses are usually met. They liberally use from the tax collections pool to pay themselves well. They extract payment for continuous world travels in search of solutions for even the most basic of problems in their own countries. They spend from the pool on programs and projects that benefit only small groups of people. They borrow huge sums and spend huge sums in developing primarily road infrastructure that is usually fraught with overrun expenses and leakages of funds fattening individuals' pockets. The road works also would lack coordination with other infrastructural entities to facilitate the running of crucial services alongside the current project, to prevent future costly disturbances to the finished work. They underspend on projects and programs for human development creating shear misery and frustrations for beneficiaries. They obviously use the people as collateral for monies borrowed, because they in turn will present to said taxpayers their need to increase taxes on even basic items, because more resources are still needed to provide better services. Even the most basic life supporting services such as water for the people, which exists in abundance, has never been met from the payment of taxes and loans, and never will be met.

Decade after decade, the collections method continues to be revised as many are accused of finding ways to better use their hard-earned incomes to better themselves instead of pooling with other taxpayers and have it wasted. Some tax dodgers as they are often called believe that paying will not significantly improve the lives of the majority of which they are a part, and they are correct. In the same breath, some managers of said system have often been accused of being recipients of bribes. They and those who bribe, amass material wealth while contributing to the poverty of millions who are forced to keep paying taxes. No foolproof solution has ever been found to mitigate against both practices and I guarantee none will ever be found under a monetary run economy.

Matthew 26:10-11 gives a very interesting perspective: "When Jesus understood it, he said unto them, why trouble ye the woman? For she hath wrought a good work upon me. For ye have the poor always with you; but me ye have not always." Here Judas, a follower of Jesus the Christ was giving the impression that money whether by tax derived from the sale of expensive products or collected from citizens' incomes as was advanced by Caesar Augustus was the way to advance common good and eliminate poverty on Earth. The oil was monetized like everything else and therefore the woman was reprimanded for wasting money by using it to anoint the feet of her Creator. Obviously, the disciples and Judas felt it should be taxed or be sold and the live cash be used to help the poor, or possibly be invested in various schemes like today's pension schemes and many others to assist the poor.

However, Jesus' statement concerning poverty clearly provided an insight into the workings of the system of taxation. Jesus knew that leaders of countries having taxed their citizens would in turn not use the proceeds to serve the interests of all citizens especially the poor but would use it to serve their own personal interests. Such was Judas' intentions. Judas sold Jesus for thirty pieces of silver. Jesus knew leaders would tell citizens that the taxes collected are insufficient to fund education for all, provide health care for all, build roads and schools for all to benefit. Jesus knew they would even conceive a way to sell the countries' resources to foreigners for large sums of money and inform citizens that the proceeds is to make up for the shortfall in tax collections and it would still fall short.

Jesus knew very importantly that money could not be and was never created by the devil to address people's needs in the first place. He knew that money could not be used to anoint his feet; it had no life, no hands, no heart as did the lady who rendered actual service to him in anointing his feet and using her hair to dry same. He knew that poverty, would result from people not having basic services such as the supply of water for consumption because there is no way money can provide such service. He knew people would not be able to buy lands to grow food to be healthy and to build houses to inhabit, because they would need money to buy but would not have it. He knew there would be constant deficiencies and deficits in a world run by money, because leaders would feed people's appetites with the lack of resources as a constant excuse for not doing good. And he knew it would be the joy of many to use his utterance, "For ye have the poor always with you; but me ye have not always", to justify poverty. Leaders then and now are saying, they cannot be blamed because they or their actions have not contributed to poverty. The irony is that such hearts are poor and the mind impoverished. It is only poor minds that create more of the same, hence poverty exists because of poverty stricken minds.

Money or the monetary concept was created and used by Lucifer in heaven. Lucifer used the concept as a medium of exchange to get the nod of rulership from one-third of the angelic beings in heaven. A third of the angelic beings voted and took sides with Lucifer to become world boss in heaven, in exchange to become his generals; in essence usurping their own Creator. This action brought about division and an eventual war where Lucifer was defeated and evicted from heaven. Where there is disunity and divisions, there is a loss of love, respect, and oneness, hence there becomes a need for some medium of exchange to create a bridge to keep a team going and to keep loyalties. Lucifer breaking away from the life source God was in essence breaking away from life, oneness in purpose, truth, love, commitment, perpetual wealth, and prosperity. Governments operate similarly. They use money, career opportunities, perks to get millions of men and women to enlist with the armed forces in exchange for their full loyalties and commitment to assist their agenda to run the world how they want it to be run. No country today is free from poverty; no country today is debt free.

The taxes imposed on citizens by leaders are also used to support the armed forces coupled with the proceeds from the sale of Earth's natural resources. Natural resources are mined by the people and sold back to the people locally and internationally. When leaders impose monetary taxes on the income of citizens and promise to use said taxes and borrowed monies to provide services to benefit the citizens and such is not done, the question of ethics must be brought to bear. Money, a lifeless object, or a thought is ascribed more importance over human beings, although, without the people's labor, sweat and blood, there could be no services provided and therefore no money. Can it therefore be ethical for governments to impose taxes on fellow citizens purporting such taxes will be used for common good when in fact the very money is used as a tool by government and private sector to manipulate the people's labor? The people are paid inadequate income that is then taxed and used to provide poor services. The people's net income is often woefully inadequate to attend to the most basic needs of the majority compromising their very survival. A great majority of taxpayers are without water supply and electricity. Those who are supplied either have difficulties paying the monthly charges or consistently have service interruption.

Many taxpayers are unable to buy healthy foods. They will often sacrifice their own health and education to ensure their children thrive. They are unable to buy land and own homes. They have difficulties travelling to work on time and to other places in their country due to poor transportation services that their tax dollars are wasted. The outcome from such a system creates a miserable network of lack of resources for the people. This in turn cause people to engage in competitions for the scarce resources causing strife, divisions, corruption, classism, racism, wars, greed, enslavement and indeed poverty. Again, Jesus was telling his disciples that they were actual creators of poverty by the very deceptive act of collecting and using money to create lack of resources so they the creators can enjoy a sense of power and superiority. How senseless is it to believe that a percentage from the income of just a segment of the working population could adequately serve the needs of the whole population? Jesus was telling his disciples and us today that people-to-people expression of love and care via work is the only way to create wealth through the willingness to serve in humility, working the hands and head and not the selling of goods for money. Paul in Galatians 5:13-14 says it this way: "But by Love, serve one another. For all the law is fulfilled in one word even in this; Thou shalt love thy neighbor as thyself."

Is it therefore moral, for world governments to force the use of money on citizens to be used as the primary tool to acquire life's necessities while in the same breath employment for all or the majority to earn the very money is beyond the governments' capabilities to facilitate? Or perhaps, is it that governments have no interest in having all citizens employed to earn money consistently?

Governments have placed mandatory bans on many things but never ever yet placed a ban on unemployment. Why not ban unemployment so all could earn the very money needed to satisfy the material needs of all people? One just must look at the countless lack of resources and realize that lack must require work to eliminate it.

Why are governments allowed freedom to manage and manipulate people's rights to have access to land and water when such belong to the people? Is this a case to examine as a defiance of ethics and morality?

In the many different eras so far, these counterfeit individuals and their allies gained along the way, continue to assume leadership positions, exerting control and restricting freedom in accessing resources that affect lives and key resources such as land, food, water, and housing. Social unrest and chaos thrive albeit being managed by lies about limited resources, coupled with the use of the state's police and military and the courts to silence people through fear and other tactics.

Although freedoms were guaranteed in the pursuit of one's happiness and written in documents on constitutional rights and freedoms such freedoms remained under subjection.

"None are more hopelessly enslaved than those who falsely believe they are free." - Johan Wolfgang Van Gothe (1719-1832)

Money and monetary policies created from the Lucifer model by these individuals were used as the tools to gain power and control to manipulate resources and citizens. One's survival is then tied to money, which first had to be earned from labor to purchase back all things produced from said labor. This money is also needed to purchase resources that occur naturally and by law, are placed under the stronghold of leaders of governments. How unscrupulous.

All countries are governed by the rule of Law; therefore, it was essential that the laws were created to support money and monetary policies. In fact, governments will say to the people that key services must be privatized after they are deliberately made to disintegrate. This is done in sweet deals cemented in law and all citizens are then required to pay monthly fees to such entities for their survival.

Whether you earn an income or not, if you do not pay you are denied life-sustaining services and the courts can lock you away for being indebted or for stealing from such entities. What horror? These entities are many, and they all have control of everything you need to survive. Water, food, land, electricity, housing, transportation, everything. So, slavery remains in tack but no longer altogether physical. Slavery in any format is immoral and unethical.

Although history has documented many protests and fights for freedom against discriminatory laws, physical slavery, laws that treated women lesser than men, laws to deny one's right to vote, the entire world remains enslaved by the father of all discriminations, the monetary discriminations firmly grounded in law. This essentially makes a mockery of all fights for freedom past and present.

Unfortunately, the use of money in securing and acquiring commodities has become quite normal to people. People are unable to imagine a world without money. Some have used it to acquire homes, an education, to pay back loans, and their material lives have improved by having money. Even the majority who struggle their entire life to make ends meet, always believe they are just a stone's throw away from their monetary breakthrough, to own their dream home or a car. Many dies never realizing such goals. Unless there is a change from a monetary run economy to a collaborative work-based economy, millions more will die without ever discovering their God given purpose here on Earth. Many send fervent prayers up to God for financial deliverance. Therefore, the entire world believes that money and monetary policies is the only formula to guarantee them freedom, equality, and the opportunity to achieve. Nothing could be more immoral, unethical, and further from the truth, although ironically, without giving the National Water Commission money, you will not be provided with water. Most people are not enlightened or aware of the lie lived as truth due to the following:

- Individuals' lack of knowledge and the greed for money to preserve their own lives (individualism),
- Pressures in life to survive causing very little interest in anything outside of instant cash acquisition to solve the immediate problems of buying food and paying bills, and for which accessing the cash, dangles within reach for many in the lottery and gambling houses. Many keep winning just enough to buy food and pay the bills so what the heck?

The majority no longer believes or is at their wits end on how to apply the principle: "United we stand, divided we fall."

Many do not know that the overwhelming incidences of illiteracy, ill health, joblessness, poverty, rampant crime, corruption, violence, and numerous other sorrows that have plagued generations yesterday, today, and tomorrow have their roots in money, monetary policies or the love of money. The system does not allow one to love life and not love money, because food, water and oxygen which is life, costs money. What a brutal trap. "For the love of money is the root of all evil: which while some coveted after, they have erred from the faith, and pierced themselves through with many sorrows," (1 Timothy 6:10).

So, in total contradiction to fundamental Biblical principles that do not support money as a tool to facilitate freedom and access to resources created by God, the systems nonetheless prevail.

Unfortunately, there is overwhelming support of the monetary system in Christendom. The clergy not just believes in the power of money for wealth creation but preaches the importance of money as a most important tool necessary to do the work of God and to spread the truth around the world.

People therefore burdened and subdued by amoral systems of manipulation and control, easily become candidates for undue stresses. Scientific researchers have documented many stresses related illnesses, which have resulted in countless untimely deaths, which in my opinion are due to lack of money. Lack of money to educate, to buy food, to feed hungry children is stress. Lack of money to educate oneself is stress. Lack of money to pay for medication at the pharmacy to normalize one's high blood pressure is serious health stress. Lack of money to pay the National Water Commission for water is great stress. Lack of money to pay rent is huge stress. Lack of money to visit the dentist for good dental hygiene is stress. Money is indeed the silent weapon of mass destruction.

Does it appear thou shall not kill, becomes thou can slowly and gradually kill as world governments trap people in their respective countries under monetary, economic, and social systems that demand payment for one's very life and get away with murder, because of the law of the land? The law of the land will send you to prison for stealing water from a shop or the water commission to save your own life. There are no laws that guarantee work for all. Working for the National Water Commission, the electricity company and the telecommunication entities does not guarantee anyone the services provided for free, although it is the workers who labor to produce potable water and the distribution of electricity. It should be free because it was produced by labor. It is by the sweat of a man's brow shall he eat bread, instead of by the sweat of a man's brow shall he be paid very little money that limits his very survival as he struggles to pay his water bill, his electricity bill and buy healthy food for consumption.

Stealing out of desperate necessity to feed, shelter and clothe oneself and family can occur when one is not paid adequately for his/her labor. If caught, the result will be conviction as a criminal and imprisonment. Such is the workings of man's laws and systems of governing.

As people become stressed from the lack of monetary resources to acquire water, acquire an education, obtain a skill for income generation, school their children, eat healthy, acquire land or homes, access health and dental care, they ultimately die a slow and painful death one way or the other. Stressed by lack, people develop cancers of different names and sizes, diabetes, heart diseases, mental illnesses and so on. What utter evil?

Do you think those who use money to manipulate and control others derive pleasure and indeed benefits from the resultant hostilities, discontent, and chaos in societies? Like Satan, they do indeed. "Single acts of tyranny may be ascribed to the accidental opinion of the day; but a series of oppressions, begun at a distinguished period, and pursued unalterably through every change of administration too plainly proves a deliberate, systematic plan of reducing us to slavery." - Thomas Jefferson. The results from oppressions as evidenced by retaliations and disputes among people, contribute to the controlled setting up of courts of law and the military forces. Courts of law and the military forces both serve as controlled platforms for handing down judgments on those embroiled in disputes. Money is often needed for the most effective representation in a court of law.

How often is justice handed down or morality upheld in the courts for those without money? How often is money and monetary policies protected, while the needs of people to live in houses, to eat healthy foods, to be treated for illnesses are not? Where is the ethics? Most judges and lawyers are slaves to unjust, immoral laws that should not have been passed as laws. A traffic judge once told me in her court that she is a slave to the laws and if I have a problem with the laws, I should go talk to my Member of Parliament. The Members of Parliament make up the government. Government makes the laws and the lawyers and judges in the courts are subjected to those laws. Did they not tell you that the executive and legislature do not control the judiciary? I guess they will say the laws are subject to interpretation.

Nevertheless, the running of the courts is financed by money which comes from the government. The salaries of every court staff are paid by the government. Interestingly, the government does not produce money but nonetheless uses money to govern and pays themselves and the courts to govern. Where does this money come from? Some comes from taxes and loans. Other amounts come from grants, selling of properties and natural resources which governments claim they own, etc. Taxations are indirect loans as organizations borrow from banks to do business. Businesses employ people, pay them and pay taxes. Their employees also pay income tax. All this money goes into the government coffers for them to manage and provide services for the people.

The government always claims the money is never enough to provide services for the benefit of the people and therefore is always borrowing more money to provide needed services. This lack of money and borrowing more money is a standard for all governments and is never ending. Lenders own the government hence the government is answerable to them and primarily makes laws to support them. These laws are also upheld by the courts. Their bosses are certainly not the Jamaican citizens. Their bosses are banks first and foremost because all monies come from a bank. Their bosses are also large businesses with lots of money to lend. The citizens work for these large businesses for meager wages. The laws offer no protection for people but rather protect large businesses or corporations such as the banks, credit unions, building societies and all capitalists who lend monies to governments, and the court uses laws to defend such corporations over people. These lending agents are usually corrupt because they demand pay back with interest on loans that they all know is the primary reason for inflation and is in fact a stress tax on borrowers. Governments are usually not affected or stressed as their salaries are always guaranteed, however, the citizens are burdened with both principal and interest on these loans. These loan sharks are always right and protected by governments and the courts. After all they are the ones that give millions to governments to run elections. People are burdened with late fees if interest payments are not made on time. They are blacklisted at credit bureaus and many are thrown out of their homes for defaulting on their mortgages with these loan sharks. The sharks are the National Housing Trust, all banks, building societies, credit unions the Students' Loan Bureau and other lending institutions.

Oftentimes, people will steal to acquire money to honor these fake financial obligations causing strife among citizenry as fingers are pointed. Some are also sent to prison by the courts for stealing goats, cows and crops leaving farmers in a frenzy. So, the loans remain unpaid, and the loan sharks are out for the kill as they engage with desperate collection agencies who are intent on licking their ten fingers when they can collect. Many cannot purchase food to feed their hungry families because they have to repay loans to these sharks who are highly favored by governments and the courts.

"To have respect of persons is not good: for, for a piece of bread that man will transgress" (Proverbs 28:21).

So, the courts are kept busy with the high incidences of strife among citizens caused from the utilization of a system that values money and taxes over humans. How unethical and immoral.

The education systems and related policies are also designed to produce ignorance and incompetence in world populations. Money is then used to generate numerous activities in programs of training, to serve as a remedy to the very problem of lacks and incompetence that the lack of money created. There is always never enough money to sustain such programs for the long term. When the money for that program runs out, and it always does, the program ends and there is a return to ignorance. What a game of money monopoly.

The control model is shuffled around. It is mainly played out in the game of general elections dominated mostly by a two-party system of control that works the model on the behalf of the owners of money. This occurs globally. People often swap one party for the other every four to five years as they seek comfort in their warped, insipid belief that the next party will be the one to govern and manage the money efficiently to make their country better again. There is not a country where all people thrive under the universal monetary economic model ordered, manipulated, and controlled by banks.

"I have two great enemies, the Southern Army in front of me and the Bankers in the rear. Of the two, the one at my rear is my greatest foe." -Abraham Lincoln

"In whom the god of this world hath blinded the minds of them, which believe not, lest the light of the glorious gospel of Christ, who is the image of God, should shine unto them" (11 Corinthians 4:4). The gospel of Christ is love for God and love for fellowmen. Sadly, what we have is love for money and all vanities over love for fellowmen.

My own experience in losing my home coupled with incidences of ignorance and lack, birthed my desire to probe the methods used in managing the Earth's resources and the impact on citizens, especially in my home country Jamaica. I desire a better formula to create equality, equity, balance, compatibility, collaboration, and fair play in human interactions.

I have so far utilized the following in my probe:

- Logics
- Engaging the minds of friends and foes
- Observing realities
- Reasoning on rights and privileges

One might argue that as ethics seeks to use reason to discover what is right or wrong, one will determine the correct reasoning since reason like conscience varies according to individuals of different persuasions, different traditions, and influences. Is there a system that can embrace morals, practice good ethics, and promote the rights of peoples, to wound the existing prejudices and discriminations in governance, and generate some unity in this world of diversities? "A good man out of the good treasure of his heart bringeth forth that which is good: and an evil man out of the evil treasure of his heart bringeth forth that which is evil: for out of the abundance of the heart his mouth speaketh" (Luke 6:45). However, "For I have given you an example that ye should do as I have done" (John 13:15).

Jesus, God incarnate came to Earth approximately 2000 years after humans had lived and reigned in a world steeped in sin and iniquity. He came and taught right living, rebuked bad living, saved, forgave, and lived the exemplary life for humans to pattern. He was also no respecter of persons as our governments are today, favoring the rich over the poor. Throughout his sojourn, he embraced everyone and never once sought to profit from anyone's adversity. In fact, he restored health and wellness to all the sick and oppressed who came to him for healing and never asked for or collected money. He never asked for health insurance or hospital registration fees. He fed thousands with five loaves and two fishes, because where there is a will there is a way. He was a skilled carpenter. He did real tangible work and there is no record of him ever using money in exchange for service. In fact, he chased the money users whose aim was just to sell and to financially enrich themselves out of the temple. He served all with humility as a true leader does. He served all, Jew, Gentile, non-Jew, and non-- Gentile. He taught, preached, and served all, withholding no good thing. Jesus is the rightful owner of all good things. We should at the very least try to follow his example. It's not too late to try.

Ultimately, the outcome of highlighting the lack of ethics and immoral laws, is to bring to the attention of all, that a moral principle of equality and access to the Earth's abundant resources through shared work and collaboration, was deliberately never factored into any man-made world economic model or in their absurd mathematical equations, in the management of the Earth's resources. Instead, money was deliberately introduced as the ultimate tool of control and manipulation for selfish gains by prejudiced groups, while creating countless miseries for many, ultimately creating poverty and destruction.

If governments were to eliminate money from the economic equation and organize a system of labor that is shared/rotated, themselves included to perform real work, such would be the game changer for a better life where people would experience what living is all about. However, to recap briefly, we need air, food, and water to live, and these are provided by the Earth we live in. Everyone needs to respect all the cycles placed by the Creator on Earth to sustain us and all life in general from this air, food, and water and faithfully guard against its destruction by replenishing and maximizing the Earth's resources for common good. It is by doing such that we will experience a whole new world of newness in outlook, discoveries, and outcomes; finally doing something different and without contradiction, realizing different results.

DOMAINS OF ETHICAL ASSESSMENT

A moral principle is an important feature of morality. As ethics probes the traits of moral principles such as Prescriptivity,

Universalizability, Overridingness, Publicity and Practicability (see addendum), it becomes clear that there are four guiding elements that influence man's response towards moral laws as well.

The four domains include Action, Consequences, Character and Motive. Action

Actions towards a particular situation often are classified as right actions or wrong actions, and reason also brings to light ambiguities in what may be considered a right or wrong action. For example, one may or may not choose to respond to a call to give a J$100 towards the purchase of food for a "hungry person". While this is a good act and is permissible, one's refusal to respond does not mean a wrong action is committed on their part because such a situation is not considered obligatory. However, on the other hand everyone is always expected to tell the truth irrespective of the consequences and this action is deemed obligatory. Here one could easily agree that the act of helping someone in need or speaking the truth should indeed be mandatory for all.

However, one could also argue, how does one determine that the individual is really in need of food? If one contributes J$100, how can one be sure that the recipient will use the donation to purchase food and not something else? One should however ask what I consider to be the most critical question: What could have led an individual to sit idle, hungry, and alienated waiting for someone to provide food in a world where tons of food are wasted daily? Why is it also necessary to exchange paper currency, which is of no value and created by some humans, for food and water which sustain human life? Without food and water, humans cannot process the very trees, iron ores and minerals built into the earth by the Creator for all, to create and print money in the first instance. Therefore, what is the reason or what has led some humans to ascribe value to money over their fellowmen and to have their fellowmen constantly engaging in very harsh, tedious, and monotonous labor to earn said money to buy back their health and wellbeing? If this is not of the Devil, tell me what is. Did not Lucifer a created being decide he the creature was greater than his Creator? Some men, obviously Lucifer's representatives have also decided that their paper creation is greater than and is of more value than God's creation of human beings. What utter evil? How destructive is this model proving to be both to the Earth and to humans?

CONSEQUENCES

The result from a particular action is always very important and therefore should always influence the response to an act, for example, lying to protect the life of an individual. If a great good is accomplished from such action, one should endeavor to do likewise to ensure this goal. One might be able to argue quite convincingly too that why not then lie your way to prosperity. While one set of ethical assessment places more emphasis on the consequences of actions in one given situation to be a step in the right direction, another still takes it a step further to offer character or virtue as the platform on which the appropriate action should originate. Lying to become prosperous in a world of abundant resources is insanity. What acts occasion lying to protect the life of another and how could one mitigate against such?

CHARACTER

Aristotle an ancient philosopher introduces character or virtue as the catalyst to engender a right response to a situation such as being honest or temperate. If an individual develops a good character, then it follows that they would not be inclined to take another's property, kill or cheat in an exam. If one has not developed this virtuous character, why then would an individual take property belonging to someone else and not expect retaliation in defense of such property? Why is it important to embrace and practice the false notion and belief that some people are born inferior and others superior? If some people are treated without dignity and allowed to become destitute, is it not likely that they will not develop good characters? Will they not be more inclined to steal to satisfy their needs especially for food and water which are like the needs of their oppressors? Character alone can therefore not be considered the basis on which to judge the rightness or wrongness of an action, since character development for all is woefully compromised, due to lack and greed. What hypocrisy to starve a plant of nutrients and still expect it to grow and bear fruits.

MOTIVE

One becomes motivated first and then follows up with action. The principle of motive is therefore advanced as an important premise on which to determine a right or wrong action. For example, if one decides to steal from the rich to give to the poor, then such action could be considered a right action. One may then argue that one could steal another woman's baby to satisfy another's desire to conceive a child and as such can be considered a good motive. I guess the child could therefore be stolen back and forth, as in both cases the motive is to satisfy the desire of both women to have children. Motive therefore seems not to be an absolute alternative on which to base all ethical assessments.

THEORIES OF ETHICS

Ethics is a system of principles that present in varying theories and deal with how humans are supposed to approach life; what is a good or a bad approach to life and how the approaches impact and shape peoples and societies for better or worse. The Ethical theories that follow should draw from our consciences or the God in our consciousness that shows us right and should in turn influence our reasoning to be proactive on issues that will engender common good instead of being reactive and creating undue stresses and miseries. We as humans are not able to use five loaves and two fishes to feed five thousand people. Therefore, we should always be proactive and ensure that we have 5,000 loaves and fishes with extras to feed more than 5,000 every time, all the time.

DEONTOLOGY

In a Deontological or Kantian System, the concept of a right action or a wrong action is predicated on one's duty or obligation to observe the rule of law. The act as described in the domain of ethical assessment takes precedence in deontology. One should therefore speak the truth because it is the morally right thing to do, and likewise telling a lie is against the rule of law and therefore should not be done.

The moral law of the Ten Commandments is a typical illustration of deontological ethic. One commandment says, "Thou shall not kill" and therefore adherence to this law is the whole duty of man and the right thing to do. If one also makes a promise to another, then one becomes duty bound to keep such promises even in cases where it may cause harm to another person. If a dying man asked his trusted friend to give all his money to the Billings Sports team of fifty children after he dies, and the friend decides to give the money to a children's hospital instead to purchase a well needed piece of equipment to save the lives of three children, although the breaking of the promise is for a good cause, deontological ethics rules the latter as a wrong act. It is always our moral duty to keep a promise.

Immanuel Kant who wears the title of being the greatest philosopher of the German enlightenment, offered both an absolutist and rationalist approach to deontology. Kant believed that we could use reason to work out a consistent, non-overridable set of moral principles. Reason according to Kant is enough for establishing the moral law as something transcendent and universally binding on all rational creatures. If one is honest about not cheating in an exam just for the fear of being caught but is instead honest from the approach that uses reasons to determine that cheating is a vice and therefore believes that it is one's duty not to cheat, then one does well as a true moral being. While this may be plausible on the one hand, deontological system would nevertheless allow for the death of three children as shown in the above example. Should one create a list of reasons for killing, cheating, stealing, or lying, it would include killing from fighting over scarce benefits and spoils, cheating to get ahead over a competitor, stealing to feed oneself or to pay bills and lying to get ahead in life. Sometimes many get loans, jobs, or entry into schools by lying. This occurs because of the prevailing systems of lack and inequities permeating societies or the deliberate decision against being proactive for selfish gains. Our manmade rule of law and guiding policies deliberately ensure poverty and use the advantages of wealth by others to control the resultant vices from poverty to feed their prejudices of inequalities, superiorities, and class distinctions.

VIRTUE BASED ETHICAL SYSTEM

The emphasis here is not on one's duty to be honest but rather on being honest because one has a good heart and good intentions. Jesus had a heart filled with good intentions and love for all and therefore was able to do good by even working on the Sabbath Day (which was considered breaking the moral law of the Ten Commandments) to offer healing to a sick person. Also called Aretaic ethics, the act of doing right is always inspired by having a good character and the desire to continue to become more and more virtuous.

In comparing virtue-based ethics with the deontic ethical system, a profound difference in action stands out. Whereas in deontological ethics, one is primarily motivated by the rule of law (legalistic) not to break a promise, virtue-based ethics is motivated by heartfelt compassion and understanding what will achieve excellence. Jesus did not break his own law but magnified his law by doing good, but the spiritually blind could not see that it is always good to do good on the Sabbath Day and any other day as well. The achievement of excellence and living well is the goal-oriented aspect of virtue-based ethics such as in the theories of teleological ethics. The goal however in the latter focuses on the consequences to determine moral rightness or wrongness.

The domain of character or virtue harmonizes perfectly with the virtue based ethical theory giving credence to Aristotle's call to develop virtuous character to ensure one's habitual inclination to doing right. Will the virtuous person of today demand that the water company designs a work program to include all persons who can work, to so labor and be rewarded with the life sustaining resource piped to every home? How else will water be piped if people don't do everything associated with laying the pipes including processing material to make the pipes? Failing such, would the virtuous person today support stealing water or food to save lives? How many people today are forced to steal to survive? What could be done to make food and water accessible to all to avoid stealing that which naturally belongs to all and simply requires labor and not money?

SOCIAL CONTRACT THEORY

This ethical theory seeks to promote equality in the pursuit of happiness for all through a democratic process of negotiations and compromises, where contractual arrangements are made and agreed upon. All are equally entitled to the opportunity to acquire an education, to employment, to have personal security, if in the pursuit of such interests, the rights of another to pursue those same interests are not trampled upon. The primary exponent of the Social Contract Theory is Thomas Hobbes who primarily addressed the idea of the political state, laws, and methods of governing.

Social Contract Theory exemplifies the act of upholding rules (deontology) for the utilitarian benefits of several of private interests. The upholding of the rules can be seen in the various organizations that delight in specifying monetary aids for specific causes or uses which cannot be altered to assist more urgent needs.

There are many flaws in the system of Social Contract, for example, if Hope's Architectural School in Bridges Town has ten available spaces for students in Bridges Town and twenty students in that community desire an architectural education at Hope's and they all meet the entrance requirements, only ten will be accepted. This in effect will deny the others the opportunity to pursue their architectural goal at Hope's. The theory while it lobbies effectively for the right of everyone to achieve their goals is in the same breath unable to absolutely stand on its own. Is it ethical to promise and promote that every child can learn, every child must learn yet present excuses of lack of resources to allow every child the equal learning experience? Many persons will never realize their purpose on Earth under the Social Contract Theory. This is a popular system used today in most countries and can be dubbed the system of scarce resources or capitalism gone mad.

SITUATIONAL ETHICS

This is concerned with the outcome or consequences of an action; the end as opposed to an action being intrinsically wrong as in deontological theories. Here the end can justify the means because persons are ends and are always more important than means. Laws are but things and means and therefore should always give way to persons. For example, in a situation where it is known that a baby is deformed in the mother's womb, aborting the child would be the most loving thing to do to avoid exposing that child to an unhappy life. To the situationalist, such a decision is morally right and therefore morals are determined by the most loving response to a given situation.

The founder Joseph Fletcher an Episcopal priest states that the only thing of intrinsic value is agape love and therefore once love is best served in an act all other principles can be cast aside. He believed that in forming an ethical system based on love, he was best expressing the notion of "love thy neighbor", which Jesus Christ taught in the Gospels of the New Testament.

The danger in espousing such ethical theory may suggest that killing or stealing in the name of love is always a right action. This is very unacceptable because the freewill of choice by the parent in the example given of the deformed baby should first be taken into consideration. The parent may still choose to have their deformed child also out of love.

NATURAL LAW

The theory of Natural Law states that human nature can determine morality and that once reason is applied to the nature of humanity and society, valid moral principles can be discovered. Therefore, as God naturally establishes the ability to reason in all men from the beginning, and that to reason is the true self of every man, it is therefore natural that man will function according to his purpose. This purpose includes the desire to aspire to one's own good and for the good of one's fellowmen.

The Italian philosopher Thomas Aquinas holds an absolutist position on Natural law, by stating that reason can always discover the right action in every situation that is also deontic by nature. However, the flaw is what happens when what is perceived as a right action leads to bad consequences, for example, refusing to abort a child that is causing threat to the life of the mother who ends up dying.

PROPORTIONALISM

Here the moral principle is to maximize the good and minimize the evil. Additionally, the Proportionalist believes that the natural law should always be upheld, however, in the interest of good morals it may be justifiable to do so just if the reason is proportional.

UTILITARIANISM

The action to which the greatest utility will be achieved is the premise on which Utilitarianism is based. The domain of consequence stands out in this ethical theory in that the outcome will always determine the action. If the results mean better for the greater amount of people, then such action is considered the right action. If for example, killing one righteous person will save the lives of a hundred unrighteous people, then it should be done, as in the case of Caiaphas the high priest granting the wishes of the Romans for Jesus to be released to be crucified to save an entire nation. Also, should one decide that it is better to give a million dollars towards the building of a primary school to house 150 children rather than to purchase homes for 50 homeless families, then such an action is the morally correct thing to do. One of the flaws with the Utilitarian theory is that it cannot guarantee that the majority will experience greater happiness than the minority. How does it determine that the 50 homeless persons will not experience greater happiness than the 150 students? Again, lack of resources is at work, which is by far man made and borne out of greed and selfishness. Sacrificing the rights and freewill of the minority to pleasure the majority, is another very popular system that is manifested. This too is utter madness.

ETHICAL RELATIVISM

The moral rightness or wrongness of an act is determined by the society from which such actions originate, and therefore what may obtain in one society may not obtain in another. Therefore, all moral principles are dependent on cultural or individual approval, and so there are no moral principles that can relate to all the various societies all the time. It is frightening to think that one could kill another out of hatred and is able to find a society to live in that upholds hate killings. This is madness.

DIVERSITY THESIS

This Thesis recognizes that moral rules differ from society to society and is branded as Cultural Relativism. The Diversity Thesis exemplifies the inclination of an individual motivation or perhaps a society at large to punish another because it gives lasting pleasure, which to that society is morally and culturally right for such action to take place possibly the last Sunday in each month. Why should another's suffering, be allowed to bring pleasure to an entire society? It is not just pleasure being derived by some, but also, wealth from the sufferings of others. This system is practiced world over and should be totally condemned.

DEPENDENCY THESIS

As a society accepts and advances a particular behavior or action, it becomes the norm for that society and ultimately morally acceptable. As one becomes a part of that society, whether by birth or adoption, one automatically espouses such morals or becomes duty bound as in deontological ethics. It therefore becomes impossible for one who is a part of that society to act outside of the norm towards a particular situation. This is an incubator for evil.

UNIVERSAL ETHICAL EGOISM

The only responsibility and moral purpose of any individual is to pursue all that will account for his own good and happiness even at the expense of his fellowman. This theory suggests that there can be lots of good to be gained by all from the desire by everyone to achieve good. The action here is always to do good for oneself; the goal is to be happy. How does this theory address the likely conflicts from two individuals aspiring to study medicine at the same institution that can only offer educational facilities to one person? Again, lack is exposed.

INDIVIDUAL ETHICAL EGOISM

This is quite a self-serving ethical theory in which the individual assumes the limelight and demands that all others are mere subjects to be used by him. While it is important for an individual to assume personal responsibilities towards achieving personal happiness, it defeats the other person's entitlement to those same rights, should for example one enslaves one's neighbor to earn much wealth despite the neighbor's misery and discomfort. No man was born for the purpose of being enslaved or to be punished so another can experience freedom and happiness and therefore Individual Ethical Egoism is not the answer.

All the Ethical Theories presented influence humans positively and negatively. However, the negatives outweigh the positives in the following areas:

- All theories except Virtue based ethics have multiple elements of moral confusion such as legalism taking precedence over human dignity

- Inherent inequalities and individualism giving birth to classism and many other forms of discrimination
- The self-serving use of love, having no regard to freewill gifted to all by our Creator

No theory espoused abundance in resources to support all humans. Instead, there is the perpetual lack in resources. Lack is the incubator for many evils as there will be perpetual fight for so-called limited resources creating perpetual conflicts.

I have also seen where one theory could serve to complement some shortcomings found in another for example, Deontology embodies the letter of the law whereas virtue-based ethics embodies the spirit of the law.

I am proposing a theory that values and respects the abundant resources on the Earth, respects all life forms contained therein, espouses equality and self-actualization of all people for common good and be the theory on which to base all ethical assessments. The theory of Social Contract in its pursuit of equality and democracy, Deontology that offers the principle of man's duty to uphold rules, Virtue Based Ethics which operates from heartfelt love and good intentions and Situation Ethics offering the strength and power of love have impacted my appreciation for the place of ethical intervention in all human affairs.

MY THEORY: COLLABORATIVE WORK BASED ETHICS (C-BASED ETHICS)

Laws are integral and serve as a guide to human interaction and development. Collaborative Work Based Ethics will not allow manmade laws to deny any person a right of access to Earth's natural resources or to be the beneficiary of all such resources. The laws will instead require organized participation of all people in harnessing resources utilizing methods and processes deemed safe, reliable and respectful to the Earth and people alike. No person will be required to use money to buy water, food, housing, and clothing, essentially buying life. In fact, money will be outlawed. No law will deny one's right to exercise freewill in the worship of one's Creator, not to worship a creator, or to believe what they choose to believe. Such worship and beliefs will not be allowed to restrict the rights and freedoms of others. Similarly, no one will be denied their right over their own body as it relates to what they choose to take in or take out. However, such right will not include imposing on the rights and freedom of their fellowmen.

Under a collaborative work based ethical system, the laws must acknowledge that the needs of every individual, can be met from the resources of the Earth. Therefore, the Earth's resources, given to all by the Creator can and will be managed to provide all people with clean air, continuous water supply, food in abundance, clothing, and shelter. No person will be denied the right to pursue their desires for a good life, which is realizing and living their purpose. However, no one will be allowed to infringe on another person's entitlement and right to the same good life whether by force, or competition to cause harm or injury. The collaborative work ethics is based on this foundation.

The pursuit of one's happiness means everyone has the right so to do, to discover their God given purpose on Earth and to actualize without prejudice or harm to fellowman. Automatic ownership and entitlement of all the Earth's natural resources, to use collaboratively via shared and rotated labor, help to facilitate these expressions of self and purpose, fairness to self and environment. This forms the C-Based ethical system.

In the event of a breach of one's commitment to the ethical system, one will become subjected to a prescribed system of reprimands. Each person will also agree that restitution befitting the breach is mandatory. An example of this, which is the most extreme and serious on the list of infractions is, if one should take another's life for any reason outside of self-- defense, or except in the case of abortion to save the life of the mother or for her own choice not to become a mother in her pursuit of peace of mind, or in the case of suicide or euthanasia, then that person's life will also be taken.

However, the alternative to hanging for premeditated murder is engaging in additional labor to support the offspring of the deceased for seven years. The affected family will be allowed 7-14 days to decide death or labor for the offender.

Currently, most of the Earth's population lives unfulfilled, unhappy, and very short lives in some instances. People are not allowed to contribute labor to gain access to the most basic needs for water, food, clean air, land, and a place to live. In fact, it should be a right for every citizen in their respective country. Citizens are denied free travel, free education, free speech. They are even denied rights to their own bodies should they decide to abort an unwanted pregnancy. This is outrageous.

Under the current system, the Jamaican state for example wishes to hold parents accountable for abandoning children. The state also says it is against the law for parents to have an abortion even if the life of the parent is at risk. It seems here that the state could be speaking from both sides of its mouth. While I agree that parents should be held responsible for abandoning their children, this can only be applicable if the child is already a registered live birth. Fetus registration does not exist. The state should not prevent a parent from having an abortion by any stipulation in law if such is considered in pursuit of one's personal happiness and which may very well lead to a child being abandoned by the very same parent after it is born irrespective of whether the child might be adopted or placed in a home. Abandoned children have lost their lives in homes destroyed by fire. The child not born from a desire by a parent to bear children, once abandoned proves the very point. One may argue that the child being aborted could have become a doctor, but it could also be argued that the very same doctor could become an abortion doctor. The child could also become a thief or a mass murderer or the pregnancy being upheld could result in the death of the mother.

The C-Based ethical theory provides an opportunity for all to realize and live their purpose. All are entrusted with the ownership of the Earth's resources, and in the same breath are active participants in caring for and sustaining the Earth.

The aim of Collaborative Work-Based Ethics is to propel a society to reason and to act with intelligence, respect freedom of will, to abhor enslavement, which should result in more harmonious interactions than currently obtains. I love St. Peter's version found in 1 Peter 2:16 which reads, "Let us simply be free as free, and not using our liberty for a cloke of maliciousness, but as the servants of God."

It is obvious from the world we live in today that the question of ethics should always be engaged in all human affairs. To eliminate the experiences of anger, lack of resources, mistrust, corruption, and violence, it is only ethical to include all people via work, to create abundance and respect through shared labor, which can only result in a united, strong, resilient, and prosperous people.

C-Based Ethics is about using the contribution of all people to achieve harmony and abundance on Earth for common good.

The workbook on bank reserves and deposit expansion entitled Modern Money Mechanics sates that; "Money is such a routine part of everyday living that its existence and acceptance ordinarily are taken for granted. A user may sense that money must come into being either automatically because of economic activity, or as an outgrowth of some government operation. But just how this happens all too often remains a mystery."

Be that as it may, it is hoped that you have seen overwhelming evidence that an economic system of money and monetary policies has not created the intended wealth, health, or happiness for most of the Jamaican population throughout their entire life's journey. Instead, the continued use of money has created stresses, miseries, pain, disappointments, and driven fear in many persons even costing many lives. The biggest damage done from the use of money is the destruction of dreams, unfulfilled dreams for not just hundreds of thousands of Jamaican citizens, but billions of people worldwide. People have remained stuck in dreamland never to translate such dreams into reality because they lack the money to go forward.

We were led to believe and still many are continuously led to believe that money remains our most important survival tool in this life. We are told that it takes cash to care. We are also told that we need money to survive. Nothing could be further from the truth.

Although we are told that water is life; and indeed, we cannot survive this life without water, we accept without any question or contempt, the strange phenomena of a perpetual reliance on this money for water. We are convinced we need this money to build infrastructure for reliable water distribution to all citizens, despite its prevalence throughout our island, land of wood and water. No one questions the whys of not encouraging us citizens instead to use available materials and to work together to ensure all have access to this life sustaining substance.

Interestingly, we are a country heavily indebted, and to date the populace is not incensed by the fact that no priority is ever given from this huge debt stock, to ensure water is piped to every nook and corner of Jamaica. No one appreciates the relevance of water to the dignity of a people. No one contemplates that it is indeed a lack of dignity in not being allowed as a matter of right, access to running water to refresh oneself and one's surroundings, to enjoy health and wellness. What is life without health and wellness? Instead, in present times the life substance remains outside the ready grasp of hundreds of thousands of Jamaican citizens. All my life, I have had recurring challenges in getting and keeping the flow of water at my disposal. I have spared no effort to conserve and pay the bills not just for the life sustaining water, but also electricity, even to my own physical discomfort and that of my special needs child. This has happened many times with us even sacrificing well needed food.

We have seen the umbilical tie of money to accessing education, food, housing, skills training, and employment and to a lesser extent clean air. All these are the very foundation to the life or survival of a people. However, with no clear detailing of our fundamental rights and freedom to life in our constitution, no one questions or demands answers on why money is used to restrict our freedom to live. No one questions the reasons why money has value but not a life.

It is always a happy moment when governments allocate money to address proposed solutions to eliminate our recurring water crisis, improve and increase housing solutions, improve healthcare, eliminate illiteracy; even when we are aware of the loan conditionalities attached. This is a yearly occurrence and failures are always experienced along the way because the money is never enough to even fix one fifth of said challenges. We have beyond the shadow of a doubt, come to recognize that money allocated for greater good invariably does the very opposite causing widespread divisiveness, leaving a trail of bitterness, disappointments, and discontent.

Money was never a part of God's plan to be used in any human affairs. In fact, the movement of money is always associated with the selling of goods and services. The selling and buying of goods and services is inextricably linked to thievery or unjust dealings. Jesus the divine source of all life conveyed this sentiment in no uncertain terms in his rebuke to buying and selling albeit within the temple of God at the time. Essentially, the trading in goods or commodities created a den filled with thieves inside the church. Can you imagine what it further creates outside the church?

You would have indeed realized, God created a world containing all things required for health, wealth and happiness and the Earth still contains all things for a relatively good and decent life for all citizens. There is no need for buying and selling anything. God commissioned us to be fruitful, multiply and replenish the Earth in Genesis 2:15. The only action required to fulfill such command is work. Work is an action word and must be used to tend the earth in every respect, with care and Godly fear for the continued sustenance of our very lives. The benefits or compensation from work are the very products resulting from work. In Isaiah 65:21-23 an example of work is given along with the benefits or compensation from work; "And they shall build houses, and inhabit them; and they shall plant vineyards, and eat the fruit of them. They shall not build, and another inhabits; they shall not plant, and another eats: for as the days of a tree are the days of my people, and mine elect shall long enjoy the works of their hands. They shall not labor in vain, nor bring forth for trouble; for they are the seed of the blessed of the lord, and their offspring with them."

It is important to understand how work can unlock and eliminate lack. Should one look at our towns, cities, streets, and the entire country today, one will see work languishing in every shape and form while unemployment abounds. Filthy streets, derelict and half-finished buildings populate our spaces. Our sidewalks are not properly landscaped and lined with shade trees and flowers to make our journey along the road light and bright. In fact, where sidewalks exist, the Jamaica Public Service's light poles are situated in the middle, hindering free movements, and posing a danger to the disabled community. Rusty zinc fences and dirty concrete walls barricade communities and homes throughout the entire island. Concrete jungles are all around. Hungry citizens are everywhere, while food is dumped after spoiling in the fields, supermarkets, hotels, and homes. Many among the young adult population are idle. Homeless people line the streets, young children and the elderly alike stricken with diseases and hopelessness abound. People live anxious lives struggling daily to buy food, access water and pay bills. The recurring story line is lack of money amid plenty being wasted, and uncultivated lands sitting idle. Many lambast farmers and the unemployed for not tapping into the production of more agricultural produce pretending that land and money are easily accessible. Hypocrites they all are. How does one describe this as prosperity?

Isaiah 58:1-7 distinguishes between real work and fake work. Verses 6-7 reinforce real work; "Is not this the fast that I have chosen? to lose the bands of wickedness, to undo the heavy burdens, and to let the oppressed go free, and that he breaks every yoke? Is it not to deal thy bread to the hungry, and that thou bring the poor that are cast out to thy house? When thou seest the naked, that thou cover him; and that thou hide not thyself from thine own flesh?" Many like to hide away in air-conditioned offices writing proposals writing the same old fancy studies on the same old issues of lack, corruption, and inefficiencies. Some like to appear on radio talk shows engaging in the same old telephone conversations with the hosts on what should be done to build the country. Politicians delights in sitting in parliament making and passing numerous laws and engaging in arguments about who is more corrupt. They all earn millions of dollars for doing meaningless work that creates more hardships than helps the poor. Is this how they display love for the poor?

So, many citizens occupy executive offices sitting around computers and shuffling papers several hours daily, then drive around in fancy cars and SUVs creating endless traffic jams. Soldiers and police perform guard house duties at prisons/lockups, drive around the towns cuddling weapons, take up roadside positions next to derelict dirty buildings or wasted land, spot-checking vehicles hoping to catch some criminals. Some police personnel issue tickets to traffic offenders assisting the process of tax collections, others pocket cash received as bribe. At the end of the month, week, or fortnight they all collect huge incomes while poverty abounds, and their love of poverty abounds even more.

Billions from monies borrowed are also spent overseas to employ citizens of other countries to produce security cameras, guns and ammunition and motor vehicles to reduce crime and violence in a country that suffers from so-called lack of cash that is needed to provide full employment to all citizens who can work. It does not stop there.

Many spend most of their hours every day working just to earn money to pay bills, while there is neglect towards the real things in life that matter. Very little time is spent with family (especially children) and friends. Parents often miss engaging one on one with the teachers of their children. They also miss out on their children's sports day at school.

And, even with all the long working hours, the bills are paid late or return every month with outstanding balances. The loss of service from nonpayment of bills ultimately results in stealing to augment limited resources. Many humans will fall to this low level when that will to survive kicks in.

There is also the constant feud among family members living under one roof due to lack of money to contribute equally to run the household. Women and men prostitute their bodies just to earn cash to raise their standard of living. Marriages also become transactional and are big business for thousands. Scamming and corruption run the cities because lack of money always translates into lack of caring. Children are sold into prostitution for cash and men spend cash for sexual pleasures from children. It takes cash to care yet nobody ever has enough cash to care. Philosopher and author Jiddu Krishnamurti said, "It is no measure of health to be well adjusted to a profoundly sick society." The population remains contented in hypocrisy and filth because every adversity becomes an opportunity to make money to improve someone else's survival.

We know very well, the importance of water to both plants and humans for survival. In fact, our very bodies are made up of more than 60% water. We must keep consuming it to stay alive. We see water everywhere, many times from leaking pipes on the streets. We have flowing rivers, streams, oceans, seas, wells, and rainfall. In fact, water is one of the most abundant substances created by God. All the various cycles and laws in nature to sustain life on Earth were already set in place by the very Creator, from the foundations of the Earth. However, plants and humans remain starved of the life sustaining substance due to a lack of money to multiply and replenish it. Farmers lose millions of dollars in crops every year due to drought, as there is no rainfall for extended periods. There is no attempt at harnessing water from underground sources and rivers unless money is available to mobilize the required work

We were created for God's glory, like it or not. How do you feel if you create a fine work of art and someone else is lauded for your work? We are to glorify our Creator through continuous worship and obedience to God's laws of love. Love first to God and second, love to fellowmen. We must respect God and respect our fellowmen. We are to be fruitful, multiply and replenish the Earth as instructed by God via work, sustaining the Earth and sustaining each other barring none.

For selfish, worthless, and diabolic reasons, the money created is used to oust the Creator out of the picture. Money is idolized, worshipped, and promoted to godly status, and like a never-ending game billions of human dreams and aspirations are crushed forever by the lack of it. Millions die annually due to lack of money to purchase food and receive medical care for sicknesses brought on due to lack of money. In fact, defeat, manipulation, and control are all part of the game from beginning to end.

Many well-intentioned persons desiring to fix problems of illiteracy, indebtedness, water shortages, hunger and housing created from the lack of money, cannot by donations of said money solve such problems. In fact, there are no mathematical formulae available or that can be invented to solve or even bring some semblance of balance to the game that is played by the creators and suppliers of money using their system of loans, grants, donations, and the payment of interest. Interest is the engine in the monetary system that creates cashless situations, ensures enslavement, and causes foreclosures, bankruptcies, loan defaults, bad credits and a perpetual indebtedness for individuals and countries alike.

Should one brave person capture all the money in circulation today and decides to repay all the indebtedness of both individuals and countries, such cash would never be enough, simply because all money owed, especially to financial institutions far exceeds actual money in circulation. Why is this so? Firstly, all moneys are created because of loans and all the moneys in circulation only represent the principal moneys captured in said loan contracts. The need to pay interest in loan contracts is the oil in the engine that works the monetary transportation system. Interest is cash that does not exist anywhere in God's universe. Principal borrowed + interest is always greater than principal hence creating a perpetual loan deficit. Therefore, new loans are always urgently needed to bridge such deficits. This leads to inflation simply by the constant need to pay interest on such loans, because interest is nonexistent. The new loans steal value from existing loans and increases the money in circulation whether there is an increase in the demand for goods and services. Then, as supply and demand find equilibrium, prices rise diminishing the purchasing power of each individual dollar and this is called inflation. We therefore always need to keep borrowing to keep increasing money. However, there is simply no catching up or bridging that deficit.

People's freedom to grow and serve is therefore entrenched in pieces of paper forever in short supply. This is ignorance at its best. People's growth and development is dependent on limited money supply. This is crazy. Without money to fund one's education, one will not excel. Without money to start a business, one will simply talk about the business plans for weeks, months, years, wasting precious time going nowhere.

Without money to seek and receive medical treatment for illnesses, one's health gradually deteriorates to a slow and painful death. The list is endless. You just try to wrap your mind around it. In fact, all the other various humbugs; the senseless killings, competitions, power struggles between men and women, political parties (JLP and PNP), and more are rooted in money. The Bible does not lie in the writing of Paul that the love of money is the root of all evil. Few people with a fervent love for money have written many evils found in societies described here. Such fervent love is like a weak link in a chain, which compromises the strength and integrity of the whole chain.

While working briefly as a project manager for the construction of an apartment complex, the developer (my employer) asked me to assist him with selling some of the apartments. He promised to reward my efforts by giving me 1% commission for the ones I sold. I sold a few apartments and when I requested my commissions, he reneged on his promise. In fact, he denied making any such promise. He was intent on ruthlessly maximizing his profit margins at the expense of my efforts. Refusing to pay me created a chain of ripple effect. Firstly, I had to further delay my plans to give my daughter another chance to see again. She lost what was left of her very limited vision during the time I was project managing the construction. I employed help to care for my child with special needs, and during my period of employment at the site, she was accidently struck in the eye by the caregiver and the retina was torn again. I had also planned to address her oral health challenges, along with other issues that required urgent intervention. Additionally, the Students' Loan Bureau (SLB) would have also received a lumpsum. Like many others, I am being pursued by the Students' Loan Bureau to repay fake interest on loans with money that I am barely earning enough of, and which I need to buy food and pay for water to survive. Without water and food, one is as good as dead. I believe many are not aware that just like fake clothes and fake foods there is also fake monies. Money is fake in the context that it is used as a tool to control resources, to create scarcities and ultimately destroy. Although nothing could be further from the truth, the SLB spreads propaganda on national radio that people like me prevent others from earning an education to survive. I wonder if all those who are not paying their water bills are preventing others from getting water to survive. I wonder if all those who owe money are stopping the minting of paper currency. Are they, by not paying the so-called loan, preventing the SLB staff from receiving their monthly paychecks? This is just another effort to create the web of lies and confusion to cover up the evils of a monetary based economic system. I and others are being labeled wicked, selfish, and evil, while money is worshipped and placed on a pedestal as the savior of the world when people are slowly, silently dying from the lack of said money. The web of confusion and lies is endless.

We saw the display of selfishness and evil presented by the devil and by the first pair of humans on Earth, and how it negatively impacted all lives in both heaven and Earth to current times. Lies and continuous distractions are used in the combined partnership between Satan and humans in the institution of money as the key to survive, resulting in a gradual transfer of man's dependence and worship of the Creator of heaven and Earth to a dependence on man's monetary creation. Nothing is more protected than money; people are afraid to show it disrespect but would disrespect their own brothers and sisters. In fact, they would hate, malice and murder their own family members over money. It is believed in almost all corners, that nothing is more powerful than money. Again, nothing could be further from the truth. We saw that Pharaoh in Egypt was not able to use all the accumulated money or riches to do the work previously done by the Israelites whom he enslaved and who became liberated through the leadership of Moses. With this absence of labor meant that production was at its end for Pharaoh and his people. Such a dilemma left Pharaoh with only three options:

1. He and his people will now be forced to perform all the work previously done by the Israelite slaves. Obviously, he had no such intention, because slave masters are usually extremely proud, reject manual labor and are incompetent and lazy.
2. Make slaves out of his own Egyptian people to work for him, which he also rejected
3. Pursue the freed Israelite slaves to have them resume real work

Pharaoh loved money and a life of partying and reveling. His money however was useless to afford the lifestyle without slaves to perform work. He needed people not paper to work so he went after people. Fortunately, he got what he deserved.

We have seen that all governments and their money producers have created the following narrative: We will only be fruitful and multiply the Earth's resources as we see fit, and this we will do by using money to enslave others to work for us so we can party and live life to the max. How many times have you heard of politicians partying and squandering money they claim belongs to you? If such money was yours, how did you end up losing control of your money for others to just party and squander as they desire? Many parties have been hosted and lavish lifestyles have been lived without your knowledge. The truth is you do not own money. Someone else does. In fact, they say the Earth belongs to them and they will control it to suit themselves. The narrative continues; we can't have everybody working and producing for common good. We cannot have everyone being able to access all the goodness on Earth. We must have power and control over our property, hence no work for humans without our money.

You must wonder if politicians are also human. They inform God that his Earth is theirs to do as they please. We will use it to create our money they say, but even better, we have mastered this so well. We administer loans in the trillions; lending what we call principal, which is to be repaid with interest. Interest is the honey in our tea. Interest allows us the pleasure to sit back, relax and sip. Principal plus interest is always greater than principal. In fact, we can create both interest and principal out of nothing and interest ensures continuous enslavement because it takes lifetimes to be repaid. So, as we continue administering loans, we will maintain full control over Earth and all that it contains, ensuring our slaves work endlessly to repay interests on loans in perpetuity.

Our money has replaced God. People have long accepted that it takes cash to care. They have long accepted that they need our money to survive and even pray to God to give them of our money in financial breakthroughs. However, readers please be aware that God always uses the heathen and their money for his glory.

The heathen says that without our money, access to water, food, housing, electricity, and transportation is next to nothing. Every day we tell people it takes cash to care, and they believe our lie. Those who disbelieve have no choice but to use our money too. They are all trapped by our money. They further inform God, that his idea of work is laughable. God, you could never be telling us to get our hands in the dirt like you did or the Israelite slaves did. To cut a long story short, with our money, we don't need to work at all. We simply institute monetary policies and rules to compel Jamaicans to work for us. This makes us all very powerful and happy. We have perfected our god that we can speak just like you did, and it's done at once. We design and use complex languages and fancy terms to perplex and brainwash Jamaicans beyond their abilities to understand how we make their lives a living hell, yet they love us and the hell we put them through. The streets are filthy, they contend with perpetual water shortages, disgusting health services and yet they are either diehard supporters of the PNP or JLP. Those who chose not to vote have no alternative but to contend with the way we run things.

Many Jamaicans subsist on white flour, white sugar, white bread, sodas, bullas, and bag juice. The sale of these killer foods puts billions of dollars in the pockets of so-called leaders of economics and commerce. The health care facilities remain in shambles and ganja smoking is high just like sexual abuse. There is violence of every type, cost of living is high and increases very subtly day after day. People are stressed on the roads, and taxi men who are hell bent on earning as much money as they can, will drive fear in other road users to earn the scarce commodity. Yet citizens all remain in sympathy with governments believing they really don't have the cash to care. One set believes the PNP cares while another set believes the JLP cares. Corruption is everywhere. Some say corruption costs the country 200 billion dollars annually. But a monetary run economy is inherently corrupt. Real care comes not from money but from people at work to serve each other.

They have also conned the people into an ideology called "socialization of wealth" to be a key ingredient to transform poverty into prosperity. Citizens have yet again been sold another lie that Jamaica is on its way to becoming a rich country using money. Nothing could be further from the truth. Our country has been rich from creation when the Creator pronounced all good. However, money has been covertly used to make us believe we are poor and indeed has made us poor both materially and spiritually.

This new lie has taken off like wild bush fire and many have started to chant prosperity because 31,000 Jamaicans transferred savings or borrowed money totaling over 14 billion dollars from commercial banks, building societies and credit unions, and credited back to said institutions buying shares in a company that produces electricity. The company then sells electricity to the Jamaica Public Service Company Limited which then sells back electricity to both the 31,000 investors and the rest of the citizens. This is one of many examples of white-collar so-called work, that produces nothing more than shuffling paper around on the stock market, in the banks and other places, while thousands of Jamaicans including many from the same 31,000 suffer and complain about the unbearable poor water infrastructure, bad farm roads, garbage filled streets and sidewalks, crime and violence. No one dares to insist that unemployment be declared a crime and that all should work to transform the entire island into the first Caribbean Island wonder. Instead, it is more fashionable to remain divided and corrupt to maintain the status quo of uptown and downtown.

Disunity and discontent in any population is an enemy and produces more of the same. I presented the amazing possibilities of a better life should we be allowed the pleasures of self-actualization so that all participate in work and discover and develop their life's purposes on Earth.

We saw how the Creator through love rescued us and paved the path of love to God and love for neighbor as ourselves, to reconnect in our journey here on Earth in radiance and glory. God Loves us and is always ready to save us despite our sinfulness. Hope is not lost.

No doubt, many might conclude that the contents of this book is but a dream that could never be considered as a workable alternative in managing a country's resources.

Dream on Cheryl, some might say. However, I would without hesitation express similar sentiments under our current economic system which elevates money over people and work, a system that uses lack of resources to force dependence of a people on money which is and must be in limited supplies. Such can never bring and will never bring widespread prosperity.

So, the constant cries by hypocrites to stamp out corruption, reduce crime and violence, eliminate hunger, rid the country of illiteracy, reduce non-communicable diseases, reduce stress and all other ridiculous goals, are tantamount to calling and wishing for utopia under a monetary based economic system where there is lack of said money to accomplish prosperity.

Implementing the alternative of eliminating money and replacing it with real work will not result in utopia either. However, when all persons are involved in meaningful and relevant work, and able to see and experience the benefits from their labor; when all can participate in multiple work endeavors, the darn devil would have extreme difficulty luring idle and lazy hands to do every inhumane thing possible to acquire money to survive. We do not need money to survive. We do not need cash to care.

I am through presenting my case, but here is the conclusion of the matter. Fear God and keep his commandments, for this is the duty of all mankind. This is a declaration made by Solomon in Ecclesiastes 12:13 and I fully endorse it. Acknowledge the source of all life. The Creator made the Earth complete with everything to ensure our survival. Our duty is to worship, honor and obey God; use the collective and rotate work to multiply and replenish Earth as best as we possibly can, for our own survival until the end of time. Will time come to an end? Yes, I believe it will. What comes after? Eternity.

ADDENDUM

Prescriptivity - This concerns the nature of morality that commands one to action. One should feel compelled to take counsel from the command or moral law for example the command to love one another.

Universalizability - This trait encourages consistency in the administration of justice in all similar situations. For example, all persons whether black, white, rich, or poor that have committed an offence should be subjected to the same standards of judgment.

Overridingness - Sometimes it may become necessary for one set of actions to take precedence over another set of actions providing good morals are upheld. One may find it necessary to break a promise such as using funds that was promised to a friend for a motor vehicle purchase to help another friend pay for an emergency surgery to save a leg from being amputated.

Publicity - This trait promotes publicity of most moral principles for people to be aware and ultimately to be guided by them. If it is the standard, which decides that one's action is deemed right or wrong, then people ought to know what they are up against.

Practicability - A moral principle should be one that allows a sense of control and balance to the agent. One should not feel any undue constraint to act within their human limitations.

Fake Loans or Fake Monies - This is the acceptance of promissory notes in exchange for credits to borrowers' transaction accounts. In the case of the Students' Loan Bureau or every financial institution that creates loans, such loans become assets and deposit payments liabilities and both assets and liabilities now rise and are entered into bookkeeping files or in computer systems according to accounting procedures and become the production of what can be described as an accounting blip on the lending entity's computer system. There was absolutely no transfer of physical currency. One cannot, just by writing numbers makes them real. This whole notion of needing money to live is unnatural, unscientific and cannot withstand intelligent scrutiny. Money has no power to create or take life. Money has no productive capabilities. Money cannot provide clean air, water, food, and shelter and therefore should not be allowed to prevent citizens from subsisting on the very life tools created freely by God for all, and to in turn be replenished by all, through collective rotative work.

Real work is the only gateway for blessings in health and wealth, not shuffling around papers in offices. Education or training must precede employment to realize efficiencies in work. So, naturally, automatically, working is the only guarantee to the maintenance and or the preservation of the survival tools for all of mankind that was made by the supernatural being we call Creator, God, Allah.

The financial institutions have in one accord, by mischief and distress upon us, unconstitutionally taken on exclusive money creation privileges, for their own selfish benefit. They collectively introduced lifeless pieces of objects called paper currency which they derive power from, using same to bend and unbend for selfish evil pleasures, as they administer fake loans, and payments of fake interests on principals loaned, creating a system of indebtedness firmly establishing slavery. How dare the SLB and their partners, believe that they have the right to demand that one must have an individual to guarantee the repayment of the loan, but cares not to be an advocate for citizens being guaranteed the right to be employed so they can consistently earn the income to be able to repay the very fake loan? This is senseless.

Modern Money Mechanics also states that the banks or lending shops does not pay out loans from money they receive as deposits. If they did this, then no additional money would be available for them to make infinite amount of loans to others, and they do make infinite amount of loans. They simply expand deposits by creating loans out of thin air.

"Until we transition from a monetary based economic system to a collaborative work based economic system, I too like all others, continue the struggle to earn money; hopefully enough to adequately acquire water, food, shelter and clothing. Any extras are always used to help my brothers and sisters do similarly."